THE BEGINNING AND THE BEYOND

THE BEGINNING AND THE BEYOND
Papers from the Gadamer and Voegelin Conferences
Supplementary Issue of *Lonergan Workshop*, Volume 4

edited by
Fred Lawrence

Scholars Press
Chico, California

THE BEGINNING AND THE BEYOND
Papers from the Gadamer and Voegelin Conferences
Supplementary Issue of *Lonergan Workshop*, Volume 4

Fred Lawrence
editor

© 1984
Boston College

Library of Congress Cataloging in Publication Data
Main entry under title:

The Beginning and the beyond.

    1. Philosophy—Congresses. 2. Voegelin, Eric, 1901–
—Congresses. 3. Gadamer, Hans Georg, 1900–
—Congresses. I. Lawrence, Fred. II. Lonergan workshop.
V. 4 (Supplement)
B20.B44 1984   193   84–13940
ISBN 0–89130–772–9 (alk. paper)

Printed in the United States of America
on acid-free paper

EDITOR'S NOTE

I am hard-put to express in words how pleased and grateful I am to be able to present to you the contributions to this volume by Hans-Georg Gadamer and Eric Voegelin--two thinkers whom Fr Lonergan has held in such high esteem and from whom he has learned so much.

The series of supplementary volumes, inaugurated by this issue of Lonergan Workshop, grows out of a long-expressed concern of Lonergan Workshop participants to open up the conversation of the Workshop to other streams of thought in theology, philosophy, the empirical sciences, and the world of practical affairs. This volume in particular is a result of the particular mixture of respect, trust, and "taking-advantage" out of which the Workshop seems to have run this past decade.

Originally, we had hoped to bring both Prof. Gadamer and Prof. Voegelin together with Fr Lonergan. But Fr Lonergan was suddenly recovering from a major surgery; and due to previous engagements, Prof. Voegelin was unable to come during Prof. Gadamer's fall semester teaching stint at Boston College due to previous engagements. In the end, Prof. Gadamer, in his unfailing kindness and patience with this organizer, consented to add a Saturday conference to his already incredibly full schedule. His extraordinary lecture, included in this volume, was actually prepared on the train from New Haven back to Boston!--a remarkable response to a topic foisted upon him only a couple of days prior to the conference. Similarly, Prof. Voegelin consented to come in the spring for a Friday afternoon and evening/Saturday morning conference, at which he shared part of the fifth volume of his Order and History (in preparation), as well as the autobiographical remarks appearing here. We are grateful to Prof. Voegelin for permitting us to print, in addition, both my translation of a previously unpublished lecture originally delivered in Munich, and also the original Foreword to Anamnesis that he translated specially for the journal, Logos, of Santa Clara. We were also gratified to find in the responses of both Prof. Gadamer, after his talk, and of Prof. Voegelin, following his talk and at an evening panel session, not only enlightening but worthy examples of their tirelessness and outstanding talent in answering questions from the floor.

Robert Doran, ever patient with the vagaries of our organizer, consented to write a paper mediating concerns of both Lonergan and Voegelin, but was unable to attend the conference in March. Patrick Byrne's brief paper reacts to Voegelin's undertaking from the perspective of the philosophy of science, and was delivered in the course of the evening panel session. My own responses to Gadamer and Voegelin are essays in the functional specialty, dialectic.

Besides the overwhelming debt of gratitude owed to the principals, Gadamer and Voegelin, many other thanks are due. A special vote of gratitude is due Prof. Voegelin's research associate, Paul Caringella. And then to different local people: first, to Glenn Hughes and to Paul and Paulette Kidder, for help with tape-transcribing, and to Vincent St John Masi for word-processing of manuscripts; second, to Ernest Fortin, Michael O'Callaghan, and Joseph Flanagan, for participating in the Voegelin panel; and, last but not least, to Pat Byrne (managing editor, Lonergan Workshop), Charles Hefling (manuscript editor), and Joe Flanagan for endless hours of work and support in the planning and execution both of the conferences and of this volume.

>   FRED LAWRENCE
>   Boston College
>   31 January 1984

CONTENTS

Editor's Note   v

Articulating Transcendence
        Hans-Georg Gadamer   1

Language as Horizon?
        Frederick Lawrence   13

Consciousness and Order: Foreword to 'Anamnesis'
        Eric Voegelin   35

The Meditative Origin of the Philosophical Knowledge of Order
        Eric Voegelin   43

On "The Meditative Origin of the Philosophical Knowledge of Order"
        Frederick Lawrence   53

Theology's Situation: Questions to Eric Voegelin
        Robert M. Doran   69

The Significance of Voegelin's Work for the Philosophy of Science
        Patrick H. Byrne   93

Responses at the Panel Discussion of "The Beginning of the Beginning"
        Eric Voegelin   97

Autobiographical Statement at Age Eighty-Two
        Eric Voegelin   111

ARTICULATING TRANSCENDENCE

Hans-Georg Gadamer
University of Heidelberg

Thank you very much. It is a strange strategy here. When I was so challenged to learn for the first time that I have to speak about "Articulating Transcendence," it was indeed on Tuesday of this week! And later, when I saw that it was not "Lonergan Workshop" by title I was really angry, because I am a visiting professor on the Boston College staff—I am not a headline!

Nevertheless I think there is a certain underlying strategy, and the formulation "Articulating Transcendence," in my eyes at least, was a provocation to tell you why I am teaching the Pre-Socratics this term, under the title "From Religion to Philosophy." And so I will try to give you in short outline what it means that the Greek philosophy is, I think, the first opening for the dimension of transcendence which has been, later, of such religious and ideological relevance.

I will begin with a short description of the role of this movement of thinking, which began in the seventh and sixth centuries before Christ, and which undeniably opened the whole way of human civilization down to today. One can debate about the wealth and the depth of many other great cultures of the past, but until this culture no culture in the Western world really covered the whole globe with its achievements and with its impoverishments. And so a question which really should be asked is, what is this way of investigation which so much changed the surface of our globe and of our soul?

To give a formal indication, what the first thinkers of Greece did was obviously to replace mythology by cosmology. This is what we see in all the documentation of this early history, and it fulfills in a way the formulation which we know from Aristotle—the distinction between <u>mythikos</u> and <u>apodeiktikos</u>, where <u>apodeiktikos</u> obviously does not mean demonstration in the technical sense of Aristotelian logic, but the more natural meaning of demonstrating by pointing to something which proves what we are saying, in opposition to <u>mythikos</u>, which itself is defined by being nothing else than the tradition: narration, repetition, and transmission of narrations—the only valid definition of myth. That means there is no other proof for the relevance of these narrations, because they are speaking about something beyond human colloquial and daily experience. Nevertheless, this transition from mythology to cosmology cannot be treated here, because in a way it remains immanence, even when there are religious vocabularies for the new vision of the universe, or when it is without age (<u>ageiron kai athanaton</u>), or when we hear something about the unmoved divinity of the universe: all that is obviously <u>not</u> opening the way to transcendence. But, nevertheless, in the background of even the greatest thinkers of this period, especially Parmenides and Heraclitus, we feel there is some motive, some experience of the futility of human life, something of this famous Pindarian statement: <u>ti to tis, ti to ou tis, thios ona anthropos</u>, "man is only the shadow of a dream; that is the life of man." The authentic religious way of transmitting the Greek culture is not through the religion of a book—there is no Greek theology in the sense of exegesis of a sacred book—but through the poetic. And in this poetic way, indeed, the finitude of human life and its involvements is already redolent.

To illustrate this background which impels the conceptual work of the Greek thinkers towards transcendence, therefore, it is preferable to use poetical documents. We can sense the experience that <u>being</u> is always also <u>passing away</u>, and that the finitude of human beings is a basic experience for the Greeks, by pointing to their attitude towards death. That they worship the dead, the corpse; that they devote and dedicate to them all their care and cult and worship, means something: a real, unquestionable excellence of human beings. Some of you may already realize that I am going to speak about Aeschylus's convenient imaginative achievement in his <u>Prometheus</u>. You know the legend. Not only was Prometheus the bringer of fire from Olympus, for which he was punished by Zeus; also, he did this together with veiling the date of the death of human beings. Here fire is a symbol for craftsmanship, of course, but Aeschylus's description of his vision is that exactly this impossibility of calculating the end of one's life really initiates and stimulates human energy, human intensity in working, inventiveness, and progress in craftsmanship. As long as human beings knew the hour of their own death, they lived in caves like animals. It is a remarkable mythical interpretation of human life, you see, that exactly this thinking beyond all limits, which has death <u>invade</u> this infiniteness like a sudden blow—that seems to me to be the first really telling hint about the experience of our limitations <u>and</u> the drive to go beyond them.

And so, I think, it is not surprising that Plato, who was especially inspired by the Pythagorean tradition, used the same myth of Prometheus. In the <u>Philebus</u> he speaks about the fact that there is another Prometheus bringing another fire; and this other fire is the knowledge of number and mathematics. That is indeed even more than that first vague feeling about the unforeseeable limitation of human beings which impels us always to look beyond our own limitations. It is, in a more graspable form, something <u>be</u>-

yond our experience possible as merely living beings. It has to do with the excellence of our soul to be cognitive, not merely a principle of life. Thus, the second point that I want to mention is the Platonic turn to the new fire of mathematics and dialectics which points to the ontological excellence of the eidetic beings or entities. As you know, Augustine really followed the Platonic hint in arguing for the immortality of the soul, basing his demonstrations on the structure of mathematical transcendence.

But, of course, how the religious background of the soul, or how the Pythagorean background of the transmission of the soul, of the initiation and self-salvation of the soul by its gnosis, is adapted to the whole Greek enlightenment and its achievements—this bristles with problems. Obviously it constituted a real threshold in human history, in ideas and in life, when the Platonic-Aristotelian turn reintroduced a certain commonality between the popular religious tradition of the cult and the new insights of the enlightenment. What really made history was not an extreme enlightenment mission to rationalize our knowledge about nature and about human life, but rather a new approach towards finding the wisdom even in the religious tradition, in the cultic tradition of the Greeks.

A point which always raised a question for me in Plato's Phaedo is the demonstration of the immortality of the soul, based on the cognitive power of the human mind and its capacity to posit mathematical entities and to discriminate them from the fugitive experiences of the senses. Under pressure of the challenge to prepare for this lecture, I saw suddenly on the train here from New Haven this morning a solution to a problem I never could solve before. In that demonstration, Plato has Socrates say, "Well, we have to prove that the soul excludes death (athanaton)." But after an argument which you may recall but which I cannot repeat at the moment, an argument about the inner affinity of ideas causing certain ideas to go together and others to exclude each other, he then says, "Well, we must now consider whether, if the soul does not accept death, it is then athanaton. For if we can prove that it is athanaton, deathless, then we also must have proved that it is anolethron, unperishing. I never understood this deduction. What does it mean that if the soul is without thanatos, then the soul is without perishing? Now I think I have it. Perhaps we can understand this as follows.

We must of course recall that something about the music of language is inspiration. When one listens to thanatos, and at the same time thinks olethros, one feels that in thanatos the whole music of the word points to something that goes up in the air, and that olethros points towards something that sinks into the dark. And it is true that the Greeks' calling their gods athanatoi, in full awareness of the futility of human life, already ties human destiny to the excellence proper to the gods, their not being threatened by thanatos. As you know, in Greek religion there was indeed a mediation between the morality of human beings, and the gods, namely, heroicization. The hero was a human who had achieved a certain immortality by being worshiped in a religious cult. Plato, for example, after his death was worshiped throughout the whole of antiquity as a hero. Whether it was on the day of his birth or the day of Apollo, there was always a special cultic ceremony surrounding the death of Plato. The point, then, is that for the Greeks the concept of thanatos already points to something beyond death.

This moves me to say that to look beyond in this way seems to me to be the excellence of human beings. We can conceptualize this transcendence by saying, "Human beings are questioning beings." To raise questions is something that is not really embedded in the architecture and order of nature. Instead it is like an outburst of something beyond the order of the instincts and drives which is impelling all living beings. It presents a new possibility, a new responsibility, and a new dimension of experience on which human excellence is based.

I should mention also that in the Phaedo life is described in the Pythagorean tradition as an ars moriendi or art of dying, and the Greek word for it was, I think, invented by Plato: thanatan. Again, thanatos. And thanatan as a word is related to other words of the same formation, for example, nozian, that is, coming about by the motion of the ocean. So indeed thanatan contains a certain redundancy, so that in meditating on thanatos we are "living through" all the ambiguity in this flow of finitude.

If we look at other statements of Plato about the finitude of human beings, the locus classicus is the initiation of Socrates and Diotima in the Symposium. There, you remember, Love is being praised in ceremonial discourses at dinner. Diotima, Socrates relates, revealed to him that all the previous praise of Love was wrong, because Love is not beautiful but rather the desire and the longing for beauty. In initiating this power, this principle of longing and desire for the beautiful, the seer Diotima says, "Well, we should see how immortality occurs. Nature maintains itself through the reproduction of the species. In human life, however, knowledge demands in the same way ongoing efforts of reproduction—memorizing, repeating, training, and so forth—rather than the possession of truths." Accordingly, since Plato the connotation of the word philosophia was not a common Greek usage. Philosophia always implied a theoretical unrest. But with Plato it became opposed to sophia, to wisdom, and meant just longing for what the gods have as their own proper privilege and possession. To be on the way to: that is the human condition. Thus finitude here is indeed conceptualized in its own positive connotations as towards the beyond.

I would isolate from this passage in Plato's Symposium at least two points. The first is the function of recollection. You see immediately that this description of the ongoing process of memorizing and training and learning, as the participation in immortality by human beings, involves re-collection. Behind recollection is of course what we call in German <u>ereignen</u>: it "comes to" us. Recollection is not what we can conclude from logical premises; it must emerge in our imagination as a re-calling—quite a nice English expression for this coming-to-us of something.

What is recollection, then? For that I should recall the fantastic and fascinating myth in the <u>Phaedrus</u>, in which the soul's destination is described —how it follows the ascent of the gods in their chariots; how all human souls choose their own paradigm and follow the way of this god or that; how the gods on the top of the sky gaze upon the broad realm of truth. But when the human beings reach this point, the horse of emotion in themselves is so rebellious that they can just look for a moment, and then fall to the earth. And in this baroque image of Plato, just at the moment after incorporation, <u>love</u> grasps the man, and he feels his wings lifting again, and glimpses something of truth again. Once more, the "coming" of a thing, and from its occurrence we have a certain access to truth, on the wings of love. I think the description speaks for itself, so that I do not need to interpret how a man in love or a woman in love sees the world in a different way, such that there is something like a fresh color in all the experiences of daily life. And this fresh color in a way compels us to something like agreement: it is beautiful; it has in a way something of perfection; the world is suddenly beautiful. What I want to point out is that Plato's whole deeper, playful imagination of this ascent to the top of heaven, and so forth, is in itself a symbol for the tendency of the human soul to seek something beyond. Consequently, in this explanation of the <u>Phaedrus</u> myth, Socrates (inspired by the Mediterranean noontime, when the cicadas are singing and he must follow the order of Apollo to let his imagination follow its own free course) says, "Well, these different representations of gods do stand for most mortals, but behind them all is the experience of the divine, <u>to theion</u>."

Notice the neuter: "the divine." I think the neuter is one of the most mysterious things in human language wherever it is preserved. German and Greek have the excellence of preserving the neuter. The neuter occurs very often in poetry. What is the neuter? To use the neuter—for example, "the beautiful"; in German, <u>das Schoene</u>; in Greek, <u>to kalon</u>—expresses something of ungraspable presence. It is no longer "this" or "that," male or female, here or there; it is like filling in the empty space. In Goethe and Hoelderlin (and of course also in their followers), but also certainly in Pindar and in Greek poetry generally, the neuter represents in a way the plenitude of presence, the omnipresence of something. Hence, the divine is indeed an expression for such an omnipresence.

Another linguistic fact also should not be forgotten. The great classical scholar Willamowitz once made the point, now generally accepted, that in the Greek language "god" is a predicate: one says about something that "it is god." A famous statement of Euripedes that I like very much runs aspazein tous philous theos, "friends to embrace, that is god." This manifests something beyond our own feeling and our own existence; something like a common sphere, as Hoelderlin describes it, is built up there by this moment. Thus, very human, completely human experiences are here pointing to this beyond, one's own self-consciousness and its capacity. To this extent, athanatizein, "to approach the divine as much as possible"—the Platonic expression is athanatizein ephroson endekitai, "to draw close to this existence of the divine as far as possible"--is an interpretation of human life.

A further point I want to make is also based on the same thing, that is to say, on the mystery of love which recalls something to us, and stirs in us some inspiration for seeing the whole universe in a domain of luminosity. A second point, then, regards the temporality of discourse. I would like to indicate, to see how in the problem of time, of temporality, the same human excellence of going beyond time occurs in Greek thinking, and in the conceptual apprehensions of Platonic and post-Platonic thought. I could allude to the Timaeus, where time is for the first time defined as aionios: a never-dying living being. Aion is the time of life, and in the case of the universe, the Timaeus states that this living being, the universe, will never die. And so aionios in this case means the Lebenszeit, the life-time, of the universe; and in this indirect form it is something like eternity in the Greek cosmological horizon. This description already points to the timeless, or over- or super-time—a first hint. I have found a lot of illustrations for it in Platonic philosophy. In the Timaeus as well as in the highly dialectical demonstrations of the Sophist there is the interwovenness of identity and otherness: exactly the discursivity of our thinking consists in that we do not open our eyes and gaze upon the totality of truth. Such an "intuition," such an intellectus archetypus as is mentioned in the third critique of Kant as an excellence of the infinite mind, is not human mind. We are "going through," pointing to something, and then distinguishing it from something else. So both identity and otherness form the structure of human thinking. Think how much time is involved in the construction of propositions, as we learn in grammar. If we follow the Aristotelian elucidation of a proposition we have the noun (the subject), and the verb—what in German we call the Zeitwort; Greek uses the same phraseology. I think in English you use an expression such as "temporal word," because a proposition is just finished when it has its time. It is now, or it was, or it will be. Any verb, then, is a time-indicator. This is of course only a most formal indication of the whole issue. But it reflects very well how human thinking in a way proceeds along its own limitations and through its own embodiedness in the course of time and life.

As we approach now the later epoch of antiquity, when the religions of transcendence were born, we have to consider the strange developments undergone by the Platonic dialogue, Parmenides. It is fascinating how this dialogue gives us almost comedy-like illustration of dialectic in treating the question, to what degree is the unit, or the One being, one or a manifold? Parmenides, initiating Socrates into the mysteries and turnings of dialectic, unfolds the following. If we concentrate on the One, then we must eliminate any form of anything else. For later antiquity, and especially for Christianity, that was of course the model of negative theology: the One about which we cannot say anything, or to which we cannot join anything—that is the excellence of the divine. So it is that the Parmenides was read in the later ages of antiquity by the neo-Platonists (followed by the Christian fathers) as a sort of theology. The One means the transcendence of being, beyond any form of determination. This is quite remote from the Platonic dialogue itself, because there the second antithesis states that Being is related to everything, so that all the key concepts of rationality can be attributed to Being.

The meaning of an antithetic dialectic, as contradistinct from negative theology as seen through the eyes of the later generations, is a special problem in itself. But the most fascinating thing is that once these two things are explained—Being abstracted from everything, Being connecting with everything—Plato breaks the symmetry of the whole book by making an addition. This addition is normally treated by later commentators as a third thesis, as follows: Being is not One; it is not manifold; it is one and polla, one and manifold. In the excursus that proceeds for some pages—one of the strangest things in all antiquity—Plato lets his Parmenides say, "Being, as we saw, participates in time, in movement"—in other words, the antithesis to the abstraction made by negative theology. But what is at issue when Being is at rest, and then changes to movement? When does it do that? What is the moment in time at which it is no longer resting, and when it is already moved? It seems hopeless to say. For so long as it is at rest, it is at rest; and in so far as it moves, then there must be an instant which is not in time at all. Parmenides then goes on to say, "Yes, it is indeed very interesting. It is a sudden blow"—metabole is the Greek work for that. It is a word normally used for the weather (especially in Boston!): a sudden change. Of course, the most notable sudden change is thanatos, this blow in which the continuity of our longing and calculating and planning and so forth is definitely closed. It is not just a matter of scholarly problems of antiquity; it has to do with our life-experience.

Furthermore, this exaiphnes, this sudden, this blow-like occurrence, opens a new dimension of time, which is called in the later terminology of the

New Testament "eschatological" time. It means a time not calculable in the chain of past, present, and future. In what is probably the oldest document of Christianity, the Letter to the Thessalonians, we have this famous exhortation to the community: Paul says, "You should not keep on waiting for the return of the Savior. He will come without your calculating expectation, like the thief in the night" [cp. 1 Thess 5:2]. Indeed, the same problem regarding the moment of the Second Coming of the Savior, the eschatological moment, is in the Gospel of John, where it is interpreted as the moment in which the believer accepts the message. It seems to me that we have a pre-shaping of all this in the dialectic of time and of movement in the Platonic view.

Strangely enough, I cannot find any trace of this whole theory of the sudden, of the exaiphnes, through the whole history of ideas until Kierkegaard. It is almost not believable! (If you can correct me, I would be very grateful.) I have asked many scholars, especially connoisseurs of medieval philosophy; I expected it to turn up in the mystics, perhaps in discussions of the moment of the union in Plotinus, which had such an impact on the whole conceptuality of Meister Eckhart, of Angelus Silesius, and of others; but this passage never occurs. In antiquity I know of just one very trivial allusion to it. There are certainly good reasons for its omission. The commentators never explained this passage, because they were only interested in the negative theology of the first thesis of the Parmenides.

But Kierkegaard does refer to it. I do not know how he got hold of it, and I am almost sure that he was not the first to do so. Hegel does not mention it as all. In The Concept of Anxiety [trans. by Reidar Thomte (Princeton University Press, 1980), pp. 82-84], Kierkegaard dedicates some pages to the phenomenon of the exaiphnes as a dialectical turning point between rest and movement, between the profane and faith. The issue is of course his whole theory of the instant of decision. The relevant instantaneity is, in a way, more than one calculable moment in the chain of nows—one now in the chain of nows, as Aristotle describes time, and as all posterity repeated after him. In the "instant" there is a special excellence; it is the opening of a new, eschatological dimension. And, indeed, that also plays a decisive role in the resuming of Kierkegaard by Heidegger. He describes existence as something which cannot be expressed as "substance," as permanent presence; it cannot be measured by calculable time, but it has its own structure of movement and of decision, so that the whole continuity of our life is not a development of time but the building-up of our continuity in making decisions. As a result, we can never recall it at will—what guilt, conscience, repentance, and all these religious things in Heidegger are about is in the same moment also the awareness of our finitude. In a similar vein Aristotle makes the interesting statement that even the gods are not able to make undone what is done.

Thus we see how the experience of Being is so closely related to this character of "instant" or "event."

I need not explain how much I learned from the later Heidegger's efforts to elucidate this "event" of Being in pointing to common human experiences such as the work of art, which certainly challenges us in such a way that we are outside time when we are exposed to its message. We are spending time without knowing it. We are concentrating on it in listening. Another example Heidegger used was the "thing"—not as an object which is replaceable and which we can buy again in the next store, but as that in which one's own life is sedimented. I once described it in a lecture about Heidegger by retelling the insight I had when he said that one cannot lose God in the way one loses one's pocket-knife. At that moment I realized that Heidegger, the young boy from the Black Forest, received one day (probably his birthday) a pocket-knife. He had grown quite accustomed to it, and one day it was gone from his pocket. This missed pocket-knife was even more for him a symbol for the Deus absconditus.

In the mystery of the world and of language we have the same thing, namely, that in a way it takes hold of us when we are taking hold of it. When we try to communicate, we are in a way listening to the anticipated understanding of the other, and choosing the word to touch him in this way.

Well, you have heard what I have to say from the point of view of philosophy, which tries to learn from its masters. How far is that an "articulating transcendence"? I would say it is a very differentiated articulating of the access to transcendence. And perhaps that is the limitation of rational approaches, which realize (and of course theologians must think so, too) that they are not the richest insight into transcendence or into the divine. I must excuse myself with the saying of St Bernard. Nihil excipitur ubi distinguitur nihil, "nothing is excluded where nothing is distinguished." Thank you.

QUESTIONS AND ANSWERS

Question: We have talked sometimes about this, and only at this time did the memory occur to me of Tillich's always contrasting chronological time with kairos. Is that the same?

Gadamer: Well, of course, it is a special use of this word, which does not really correspond to the use of it in antiquity. Tillich was not a classical scholar like me. And, you know, kairos occurs of course in the Greek, and it means the right moment for something.

Question: The opportune moment.

Gadamer: Yes. And to this extent it is similar, but he was of course also inspired by Kierkegaard, using the lighter fashion of his own flexible intellect. I am inclined much more to go step by step.

Question: In reading Gadamer and in reading Foucault, I have an impression that their theses are contradictory. Am I right in this impression? The impression that you would stress <u>connaissance</u>, where Foucault places his entire emphasis, in <u>Archeologie de Savoire</u>, on <u>savoire</u>—on a maximum objectivity. Do you feel yourself at an opposite pole from Foucault, or are there points of similarity?

Gadamer: Well, this question I am not able to answer: my acquaintance with Foucault is insufficient. One is, as you can imagine, very selective. When I wrote my book I was already sixty. And, you know, this very human process of having a resonance with the voices of others becomes smaller and smaller with the advance of years. So in reading books of the French thinkers, I read where I had the most resonance. So I am much more acquainted with Derrida than with Foucault. But you must excuse my limitations. I spoke about the finitude of human beings.

Question: Did I correctly understand you to say that the understanding of "instant" by Parmenides is very similar to the understanding of "instant" by Kierkegaard? If that is so, how great was the influence of Judeo-Christian revelation upon Kierkegaard's understanding? How great a differentiation would there be, if any, between Parmenides's understanding of "instant" and Kierkegaard's understanding, when the meaning of presence in the cases of Plato and of Judeo-Christian revelation would seem to be different?

Gadamer: The question is very good. Well, certainly, the astonishing fact that I observed is that it is just Kierkegaard who uses this notion of the Platonic Parmenides. Why did he go back to the Platonic-Parmenidean dialectic?

It of course comes up in the course of the polemical opposition to the total mediation of philosophy and religion by Hegel. He perceived that to be his challenge; his "either/or," his whole approach to his own existential problems of the believer was also at issue in his disagreement with the Lutheran state church. His question was, how can I overcome this overdone mediation which gives us the impression—and, you know that is really hard in Hegel—that even resurrection is happening every moment in the development of insight in human beings? This whole extremism of Hegel's spiritualistic metaphysics—this Joachimism in Hegel—is I think what inspired Kierkegaard to use this Platonic form of dialectic as a means of resistance. He makes reference to the "instant" in Plato, to this unmediated, unmediatable jump, in order to interpret the "leap of faith." One can debate the validity of this form of theological self-interpretation in Kierkegaard, but his exact motivation is beyond question.

Question: I find it interesting that you should say this of Kierkegaard in relationship to Plato's <u>Parmenides</u>, because it seems to me that certain Protestant scholars like Emil Brunner would be inclined not to accept such an interpretation, since it represents an insertion of the <u>logos</u> of philosophy; whereas it would seem to me that he is claiming that Kierkegaard was attempting to go to a biblical form of <u>logos</u> to deal with that question. And yet you were making the connection between Kierkegaard's "instant" and Parmenides's "instant". Maybe I should understand that in terms of motivation.

Gadamer: Well, certainly you are completely right. The whole story is recurring again, when we are speaking about the reinterpretation of, or the use of, Kierkegaard by the post-Barthian theology. I am much more acquainted with Bultmann; but I can demonstrate very well how, for Bultmann, the eschatological time was so predominant that he almost dissolved the whole <u>narrative</u> layer of scripture in his appeal to the eschatological moment. I told my students one day about participating in Bultmann's lectures on the exegesis of John, during the period of his greatest extremism, when he was so fond of the eschatological moment that he even risked dropping all the farewell discourses—because a return of the Savior after saying farewell would have been calculable time and not the eschatological time which is happening at every moment. Of course that, I think, was a lack of hermeneutical skill for Bultmann failed to realize how different genres of speaking occur in the Bible. Narrative passages like the farewell discourses, of course, indicate another form of temporality than, for example, Paul's Letter to the Thessalonians, who are aware that he is really pointing; also the Gospel of John, in some parts of the prologue, and so forth.

I am far from going into the details of the theological application. Nor does Kierkegaard seem very defensible as a theologian. His contribution was to oppose the Hegelian mediation of everything. And in that respect he has a very important place, even for theologians; but I think it has become clear, especially in our century, that the theology based on Kierkegaard remains one-sided.

Question: Professor Gadamer, I was struck by your analysis of the power of the neuter, and it strikes me that one thing that makes a reader familiar with the history of Christianity uncomfortable with Heidegger is, he seems to listen more to the voice of the Greeks, in the emphasis on the neuter, than to Kierkegaard, who would never construe the Absolute in terms of the neuter. And yet, Heidegger borrows themes like "gift," and so forth, from the Christian tradition. Do you see him as trying in any way to rethink some of the Christian themes with emphasis on the power of the neuter?

Gadamer: Surely, the later Heidegger tried very often to approach the real religious things with the help of the neuter—when he speaks about das Heilige, when he tries to bring together the whole and the holy, and such little mysterious things in his later writings. Or when he quotes Hoelderlin with the question--and there I think is the indirect answer to your question. He once interpreted one of the latest texts of Hoelderlin, and arrived at the formulation: "Who is God? That is perhaps beyond the possibilities of our asking. But what is God? That we should ask." You see how he indeed perceived and made a limitation there. I think it is a quite Husserlian problem to say, "We cannot go beyond that without revelation." The views of rational theology, even of some dogmatics in Christianity, go so far as to say that we cannot really interpret the Trinity by rational means alone, without revelation. But I think this is recognized by all the confessions, and Augustine was well aware of the purely preparatory function of his speculations about the Trinity—they have nothing to do with real dogmatics. They amount, I think, to twenty years of interpretation of the Trinity.

But as regards the other question—how far a personal God can be explained by the theologian or the philosopher—I believe there is a disagreement between Unitarians, at least, and the Catholics, as far as I can see. But that is quite beyond my competence. I can just go so far as I tried to follow the Greek questions.

LANGUAGE AS HORIZON?

Frederick Lawrence
Boston College

INTRODUCTION

The title, "Language as Horizon," shorn of its question mark, expresses a critical insight that emerged from a key transition within the context of continental philosophy. The transition to which I am referring occurred in the course of the revolt from the once dominant neo-Kantian philosophy known as "the phenomenological movement." The Husserl-inspired return to the things themselves issued in a phenomenology which concentrated on or took its bearings from the experience of immediate sense perception, prior to any classificatory or categorizing schematisms. Yet, as both Scheler and Heidegger made clear, pure perception is at most a limit phenomenon, hardly ever ostensible within concrete human experience. Normally, sense perception occurs within an as-structure, and so objects of sensation are rarely just registered upon our sense organs without simultaneously being taken <u>as</u> something or other. As human beings, therefore, we concretely and actually have our world as worded, on the one hand—the <u>Sprachlichkeit der Welt</u>. And on the other hand, as human beings we performatively have our words as "worlded"—the <u>Sachlichkeit der Sprache</u>. The upshot of this, to make an oversimplified story shorter, is that the phenomenology of perception has become increasingly displaced by a linguistic—or as it is usually called—a "hermeneutic" phenomenology.

Hermeneutic phenomenology examines the range of human action—from the most primitive signs of consciousness to speech, decision, and deed—as it occurs within the medium of language; as mediated by language; as intrinsically linguistic. To use a somewhat different vocabulary, once one learns one's mother tongue, one's conscious activity is almost never a matter of sheer immediacy; instead one is always operating in a world mediated by meaning.

Hermeneutic phenomenology's way of approaching language differs from approaches of most versions of structural linguistics which tend to isolate language as a repertoire of signifiers and rules from its concrete use in speech. For Gadamer, in fact, the privileged data on language are to be found in the performance of conversation. In short, hermeneutic phenomenology is a comprehensive reflection upon the way human beings make sense of their lives conversationally. Conversation is both its privileged theme and its characteristic method or mode.

RORTY'S SCEPTICAL DERAILMENT OF HERMENEUTICS

One reason for the question mark in the title is that Richard Rorty has published a currently rather influential book entitled <u>Philosophy and the Mirror of Nature</u>. He has followed it up with several articles repeating and spelling out his message in journals as diverse as <u>The Review of Metaphysics</u>, <u>The American Scholar</u>, and <u>The New Republic</u>. The prose of Rorty is limpid, graceful, and a delight to read. It combines broad knowingness with an aura of carefully weighted sophistication. The book gives us an interpretation of the current situation of philosophy. It takes the form of a somewhat chronologically and elenchically ordered reconstruction which I think is a cross between history of ideas and sociology of knowledge (or ignorance, as the case may be). Rorty is constantly correlating authors' ideas about philosophy (his own included) with their social and institutional "job descriptions." The gist of his message is quickly conveyed by the title of his seventh chapter, "From Epistemology to Hermeneutics": epistemology is over; hermeneutics is in. Let me briefly describe Rorty's line of argument.

Before doing so, however, it is well to recall that ancient philosophy's desire to give an account of the cosmos, by replacing opinions or myths about what is highest and best with true and certain knowledge about beings by their causes, eventually devolved into the question about being as first philosophy. But in time, the answers to the question about being expounded by the various schools made first philosophy (or metaphysics or ontology, as it came to be called) controversial in the sense that the question about being actually turned into a series of disputed questions which could never hope to end as long as no basis for their resolution could be agreed on. It remained for the rise of modern science, along with the Machiavellian revolution in morality, with which the new science's most influential proponents, Hobbes, Bacon, Locke, and Descartes were involved, to bring about a displacement of the question about being from its position of primacy. The question about knowing—epistemology—became the first official task in philosophy's order of business.

Rorty conceives of epistemology in Cartesian or Kantian fashion as 'foundationalism': it is to provide grounds, true and certain—indeed, unshakable—foundations, not merely for its own knowing but for cognition on the part of common sense and every bit as apodictic as the <u>episteme</u> that Aristotle in his <u>Posterior Analytics</u> conceived to be the goal of the noetic quest. Moreover, such foundations would be attained by "the mirror of nature," whether as Descartes' <u>res cogitans</u>, Locke's <u>tabula rasa</u>, or Kant's

Ich denke. Epistemology, therefore, means the historical trajectory of thought which has sought to answer the question about knowing by demonstrating how either or both the most obvious features of human knowing—namely, sense perception or intuition on the one hand, and words, terms, names, or concepts on the other—yield a reflection inside us that corresponds with reality outside. According to Rorty, epistemology's favorite and recurrent strategies have tended to try to isolate "privileged representations" purified of imaginative distortions either by means of an ever so pure perception of what is really out there and nothing else; or by way of the commensurability of one's concepts with some criterion susceptible of algorithmic formulation.

Although Rorty repeatedly concedes that the fate of epistemology has been realized long since by the likes of Wittgenstein, Dewey, and Heidegger, he has felt himself called to assemble revisionist accounts of a host of contemporary thinkers to lend greater plausibility to this verdict.

Thus, to give a drastically oversimplified summary:

(1) There is no "given" or "fact" to be perceived and so no pure perception or tokening of it (Sellars's "myth of the given").

(2) It is not possible to discriminate language from fact (Quine's "inscrutability of reference").

(3) The impossibly Quixotic appraisal of meaning in terms of reference has to give way to sensible laying out of the syntactical context of words by which the whole of one's language specifies what determinations and inferences are warranted (Davidson).

(4) Following Wittgenstein's dictum of not speaking about what we know nothing about, let us eliminate all speech about mind, mental acts, and so on (Malcolm, Ryle).

(5) The business of knowledge ultimately resolves into <u>either</u> conventions of language or symbolization to which we or our particular tribe or milieu are already accustomed and habituated (normal language or science); <u>or</u> novel and revolutionary conventions (abnormal or revolutionary language or science) (Kuhn).

In sum, epistemology has not delivered a satisfactory answer to the question about knowing up till now, and it will never be capable of delivering it, either.

On the basis of this construction of these thinkers, Rorty thinks he has shown that the assumptions upon which the question about knowing perennially has been based have been successfully debunked. And to him has fallen the task of announcing the good news that when philosophy got into the business of epistemology, it invented a bunch of pseudo-problems. Furthermore, he is also here to announce the bad news (or good news, depending on how you look at it) that when those pseudo-problems are dissolved, the rationale for philosophy as an independent discipline gets displaced into the hermeneutic dimension of disciplinary or commonsense conversations.

So it is that the question mark in my title was partly motivated by my conviction that Rorty has gravely distorted the point of hermeneutic philosophy. For you see Rorty is not merely content to claim the "truth is not the sort of thing one should expect to have a philosophically interesting theory about"; he is plumping for a post-philosophic culture "in which no one—or at least no intellectual—believes that we have, deep down inside us, a criterion for telling when we are in touch with reality or not, when we are in the truth."

But I suspect that when Gadamer warns us that salutary truth of genuine insight has been in danger of being sacrificed on the altar of "method"; or when a Heidegger claims that in the wake of Descartes, modern philosophy has tended to be more interested in certitude than in truth—in either case, both men are still interested in truth in the sense of knowing what's what, even if both regard what Zeller labelled <u>Erkenntnistheorie</u> as an unfortunate waylaying of the truth question. So in this paper I contend that it is one thing to set right a distorted or woodenheaded view of truth as correspondence by a phenomenological breakthrough to language as horizon. But it is quite another thing to agree with Rorty that honestly acknowledging the "ubiquity of language" is tantamount to admitting that philosophy "cannot answer questions about the relation of the thought of our time—the descriptions it is using, the vocabulary it employs—to something which is not just some alternative vocabulary" (Rorty, 1982:32). If epistemologists have managed to misunderstand the question about knowing, this does not mean that it cannot be correctly understood and posed. More simply, if knowing is a self-correcting process—as hermeneutic philosophy supposes it shall ever be here below—this does not imply that such "correcting" is ultimately just an arbitrary choice of a new perspective, "a slow and painful choice between alternative self-images" (33). Yes, the metaphor of "holding up the mirror to nature" may be misleading; the equation of knowledge with either unadulterated sense perception or some explicitly putative intuition of concepts or a reduction to some explicitly formulated first propositions may be as wrong as can be; but that does not warrant Rorty's blatantly Nietzschean assertion that there is "no criterion that we have not created in the course of creating a practice, no standard of rationality that is not an appeal to such a criterion, no rigorous argumentation that is not obedience of our own conventions" (32).

I suggest Rorty's contention that philosophy has become "conversational" instead of "foundationalist," and "edifying" instead of "systematic" only stands in apparent agreement with the therapeia for modernity proposed by Gadamer's hermeneutic philosophy. I hope by the following account of that therapeia to show how hermeneutic philosophy's breakthrough to language as horizon may be dissociated from the benevolently nihilist implications Rorty draws from "the ubiquity of language."

GADAMER'S THERAPEIA

Therapy for any pathology requires a diagnosis as well as some suggested strategy towards a return to health. Let us examine first the diagnostic and then the antidote.

A. Diagnostic:

I would begin by stressing my agreement with Rorty that "the overcoming of epistemology through phenomenological research" and especially by Heidegger's project of a hermeneutic phenomenology is a central concern of Gadamer's philosophy. Elsewhere I have tried to show how in <u>Wahrheit und Methode</u> Gadamer used a critique of Kant's aesthetic philosophy and of the epistemologically oriented articulations of the cognitive status of the <u>Geisteswissenschaften</u> to elaborate a diagnosis of the pathology of epistemology. Key terms in Gadamer's diagnostic are "the nominalist prejudgment" and what Heidegger in <u>Sein und Zeit</u> characterized as the "horizon of <u>Vorhandenheit</u>." I think it can be shown through a careful study of the works of both Heidegger and Gadamer that both these clues may be fairly translated into a set of typical mistakes or oversights. They may also be dismantled or debunked through a painstaking application of their style of phenomenology of conscious intentionality. Thus, for Gadamer and Heidegger, epistemology since Descartes and Locke has fallen prey to a set of oversights regarding what actually takes place when we think we are knowing. And these oversights do correspond rather remarkably with Rorty's brief against epistemology in terms of "the mirror of nature."

By the "nominalist prejudgment" and the "horizon of <u>Vorhandenheit</u>," then, is meant the following network of assumptions in cognitional theory:

(a) <u>Abstract deductivism</u>: an overweening concern for the logical model of subsumption or syllogistic reasoning together with an exaggerated estimate of the need for apodicticity or the requirements of universality and absolute necessity.

(b) <u>Conceptualism</u>: a preoccupation with the universality and necessity proper to concepts, words, terms, or names which often accompanies the assumption that concepts arise unconsciously, for example, the Scotist view that knowledge is primarily intuition, producing a perfect replica of a universal <u>a parte rei</u>, in order to be intuited intellectually as regards their mutual compatibility or commensurability, or applied or fit onto the world out there in some sense (Sala, 1971, 1974).

(c) <u>Perceptualism</u>: the conviction that knowing <u>tout court</u> basically either is or has to be like taking a look at what is already-out-there-now (Sala).

(d) <u>Reification of consciousness</u>: the literal application of spatial metaphors to the process of knowing based on the conviction that consciousness is a container of some sort.

When these kinds of assumptions are at work, the question of epistemology, How do we know? is misunderstood along something like the following lines: How can subjectivity dwelling within itself (<u>res cogitans</u>, and the like) be sure it gets out to, and brings back in, what is really existing out there (<u>res extensa</u>, and the like)? The following implications go along with this:

(1) the primordiality and ultimacy of the subject/object split;

(2) a model of the knowing subject who:

(a) disposes instrumentally of ideas, representations, impressions, etc. in isolation from any world;

(b) knows best and perhaps only what itself (<u>verum et factum convertuntur</u>), and so whose reflective activity is chiefly technical and calculative;

(c) is beset with the problem of deciding whether its immanent creations have an actual reference to the 'real out there';

(d) can know itself only as an object distinguishable from other objects only as being present in an immediately evident way.

Such then is the core of a diagnostic worked out by hermeneutical phenomenology. In what follows, I shall speak of this cognitional and epistemological sickness as "picture thinking."

B. Therapy:

When, to echo Heidegger, technology has become the ontology of our age; or, to borrow from Habermas, science and technology have become the background ideology of modernity, then it is understandable that Gadamer's concern to overcome epistemology bespeaks less a preoccupation with epistemology than the recognition that it plays a key role in his overall intent to care for the mediation of truth in history by countering the modern dominance of scientism and methodolatry. But precisely this overall intent and the way he has sought to execute it show why Rorty's interpretation of hermeneutics is abortive.

One way of characterizing the project of hermeneutic philosophy is to appeal to what Gadamer has in the last decade or so been trying to convey regarding Heidegger's impact on him. It has to do with his realization that the prime analogate for the Hermeneutik der Faktizitaet is really Aristotle's practical or political philosophy. Heidegger radicalized Husserlian phenomenology by thematizing the Als-Struktur of Vor-Struktur of Dasein's conscious intentionality: we exist or live by interpreting our already situated being-in-the-world. Primary for Heidegger were not the objects of sense perception or human being as abstract or per se, or as grounded on necessity and yielding absolute certitude, but the pragmata: the things we handle and with which we are concerned as already located within universes of discourse. In other words, hermeneutic philosophy gets started by making sense of the way we make sense of our lives.

Similarly, Greek philosophy began with the practical or political problem of the right way to live. And for Aristotle, this question was taken up not by "theoretical science" in the strict sense, but by practical or political philosophy. By reflecting on the good or bad performances, regimes, ways of life; by thematizing what makes something choiceworthy as a matter of fact; and by justifying the autonomy and legitimacy of such a task, Aristotle provided an example or rationale which clarifies the nature of hermeneutic philosophy (Gadamer, 1981a, b, c,).

The practical or political question has to do with judging the way one makes sense of one's life. This is the mother-lode or matrix of hermeneutic philosophy's recovery of the truth-question both from epistemology and from technical and scientific dominance. Wahrheit und Methode shows how creating or appreciating a work of art, writing history or carrying out any scholarly investigation are not separated from the finite acts, attitudes, and orientations by which I take up a direction for my life. Indeed, truth is at stake in such enterprises. But what is meant by truth here is not primarily faithful description or correct understanding—although Gadamer does not mean to denigrate, disregard, or shirk these dimensions. It is rather truth in relation to Aristotle's ta heneka: that for the sake of which everything else is chosen; or, as we would be more likely to express it, what gives meaning to my life. Taking up a way of life means accepting it as true or truly good. Judging the truth of one's life or existence differs from judging the truth of statements because the former sort of judgment actually involves a complex set of operations summarily expressed by Aristotle's practical syllogism: apprehending an end, consenting to it, deliberating concerning means, and choice of the means. A direction in life or a way of life is true, to the degree that it contributes to one's excellence or, as we would say today, one's genuine development and authentic selfhood. Hence, the overwhelming importance for Gadamer of Aristotle's accounts of phronesis or physei dikaion.

Just as Aristotle's ethical reflection starts with mature, well educated, and well bred people, so, too, Gadamer's hermeneutic reflection is actually explicitating his personal performance throughout a lifetime of scholarly research and teaching as well as the shared ethos lived out within an institutional framework which, despite its shortcomings, made possible relationships among an elite that included teachers like Cohen, Natorp, Hartmann, Friedlaender, Bultmann, Heidegger, and peers like Jacob Klein, Leo Strauss, Gerhard Krueger, Karl Loewith, Helmut Kuhn, and so on (Gadamer, 1977). Just as in Aristotle deliberation and decision are decisively conditioned by one's character or background, so too the experiences of art and of reading great texts bring out and depend on the intimate connection between one's capacity to learn and what one has been becoming. Finally, just as in Aristotle the judgment regarding alternate ways of life (as based on pleasure or nobility or intellectual virtue) cannot be adequately asked without also engaging the question of the best regime or way of life of the political community, so, too, hermeneutic reflection which makes sense of the way human beings make sense of their lives cannot but engage language as the trans-subjective medium of the moral style of a community's words and deeds. Hermeneutic phenomenology acknowledges the manner in which the language of the civilis conversatio bestows upon the members of a speech community the truth of its direction, so that a proposed way of life as shared or personal cannot be fully assessed unless one lives it.

To summarize then, hermeneutic philosophy as therapy for modernity is a transposition into the contemporary situation of Aristotle's practical and political philosophy: it is showing the pervasiveness in all fields of human endeavor of the mutual mediation of knowing and choosing ends and means which Aristotle spoke of as getting performed concretely by phronesis—the delicate, undogmatic application of an already extant syntheke to a concrete situation that yields a normative moment without akribeia (Lawrence).

THE CONVERSATIONAL NATURE OF LANGUAGE AS HORIZON /1/

Heidegger succeeded in dismantling the knowing subject of Cartesian epistemology and in relocating the subject within language as the house of being. The result was not without its difficulties insofar as in the course of this relocation the human subjects tend to get relegated to the role of subordination to a fateful dispensation. Again, Rorty shatters the speculum mentis and announces the advent of a post-philosophic culture in the name of the ubiquity of language. But I would argue that a key to the ambiguity of Heidegger's conception of language as horizon is his suspicion of questioning. In like manner, a clue to Rorty's mistake is that he simply sets conversation in juxtaposition to inquiry. In contrast, Gadamer "approach[es] the obscurity of language from the vantage of the conversation that we are" (1965: 360; 1975:340). It is the securing of the notion of language as horizon to the dynamic structures of the conversation that recommends Gadamer's conception instead of the others.

Gadamer's analysis of hermeneutic experiences as an actuation of wirkungsgeschichtliches Bewusstsein culminates in a description of conversation. When we turn to his discussion, we find that Gadamer begins from the insight that the experience of the Thou presents itself as a prime analogate for the experience of tradition. He distinguishes three types of Thou-experience.

A. Conversation:

A first type of Thou-experience abstracts from the behavior of its fellow beings typical traits, gradually building up a knowledge that can be called upon precisely for the purpose of using one's fellows. It is an utterly egoistic way of experiencing the Thou; a way that directly contravenes Kant's famous imperative that persons ought always be regarded as ends, never as means to some end outside themselves (1965:34; 1975:322-323).

A second type of Thou-experience would be aware of the reflexivity and mutuality of the I-Thou relationship, but still remain calculatingly egocentric in the pretense "of already knowing the claim of the other, indeed, even of understanding the partner better than she understands herself" (1965:341; 1975:323). The effect of this mode of experiencing the Thou is to "take from the partner any legitimacy for her own claims" (1965:342; 1975: 323). Gadamer calls this "a reflective form of striving for domination"— which at once serves to fend off from oneself the claim of the other.

A third and more genuine experience of Thou is one in which we do not already know the partner's claim and therefore we allow him or her to say something to us that we might not have known before. This implies a fundamental openness, which, paradoxically enough, is personal almost by being impersonal: this openness is so basic that it "includes the recognition that I must interiorly let something hold good against myself even if there were no other partner present who was actually making it hold true in opposition to me (1965:343; 1975:324). In other words, according to Gadamer, we only allow others to be themselves in the act of letting them have something to say—not simply in letting them have a voice, but also in granting them a hearing: "Belonging together (Zueinandergehoeren) always means at the same time being able to listen to one another (Auf-einander-Hoeren-koennen)" (1965:343; 1975:324).

B. Conversation as Dialectic:

But for Gadamer it is the model of the Socratic dialogue which is the exemplar of conversation. The maneuver of doubling back and examining one's assumptions and attempting to force them to their consequences is something we rightly associate with Socrates and Plato and that particular form of friendly conversation called dialectic. Socratic dialectic attempted to lay bare the conditions for rational discourse in the face of the power of the comprehensive outlook at work in the background of every person. This outlook which shapes our understanding of basic matters has gradually co-agulated out of everything we have seen, read, and been told about from the time of our birth. The overarching convictions or 'sense of reality'—one might with justice even say, the catchwords by which we live—often or usu-ally answer the concerns that are other and often more powerful than the concern for true meaning and value; and yet at the same time they are sub-terraneously linked with that concern. Indeed, the dialectic of Socrates appeals to that latent link, and uses it to correct and purify that compre-hensive view. So Socratic-Platonic dialectic is the path from the primary, undifferentiated and ambiguous outlook to an adequate view of reality. The heart of the process of dialectic is both the heart of the attainment of know-ledge in general as well as the driving power behind any genuine conver-sation of dialogue: asking questions (Burrell).

Socratic-Platonic dialectic, then, is conversation in the mode of Besinnung, of heightened awareness. In it Gadamer sees an indissoluble connection between the art of holding a conversation, the art of thinking, and the art of asking ever further questions (1965:349; 1975:330). By "art" in all these instances, of course, Gadamer does not mean a skill (techne) that is teachable and learnable in the manner, say, that carpentry is. Why? On account of the role asking further questions plays in each of these activi-ties—since questions arise in an utterly non-manipulable fashion. Questions, in order to be posed, first have to occur to one. Now while it is characteristic, of Socratic-Platonic dialectic to be concentrated upon the issue in the middle of the table, the key to any partner's participation in what is moving in and through the conversation is the exactly the "determinate nescience" (<u>bestimmtes Nichtwissen</u>), the known unknown, the <u>docta ignorantia</u> proper to questioning (1965:344, 348; 1975:326, 329).

Moreover Gadamer reminds us, thinking and knowing (<u>episteme</u>) are dialectical in nature precisely because their occurrence depends on one's penetration beyond <u>doxa</u> (the taken-for-granted, the obvious, the established [1965:348; 1975:329] or fixed opinion [1965:349; 1975:330]) to hypothesis (i.e., the range of alternative and possibly relevant answers <u>as only possibly relevant</u>). This penetration is permitted solely by "laying out the issue in the openness of a particular perspective, angle, or direction of inquiry and reflection" (1965:346-347; 1975:327-328).

"Hitting upon" the right answer, the correct understanding of any given issue, therefore, is revealed by Socratic-Platonic dialogue to be less a matter of one's being clever at "giving answers" than the infinitely more difficult ability to really ask questions (1965:345; 1975:326), to suspend a subject matter in its possibilities among various alternatives.

The reality of dialectic makes unmistakable the strict correlation between the exigencies of the subject matter of discourse and the discipline of questioning openness. This correlation underlies the apparent impersonality at play in the third, authentic sort of Thou-experience described above. For it determines the dynamics of mutual respect and self-realization of partners in a conversation. The all-too-common "talking-past-one-another" of many 'conversations' is not necessarily overcome by the "turning-towards" (Buber's <u>Hinwendung</u>) of partner to partner—for this, as I have remarked in relation to the second sort of Thou-experience, is not necessarily incompatible with managing the conversation to one's own ends and with manipulating one's partner. For Gadamer, what is most likely to ensure that one is talking "for" and "with" the partner—is subordinating oneself to the tutelage, the leadership, the guidance of the subject matter to which the partners in the conversations are oriented (1965:349, 360, 422; 1975:330, 341, 404). Then it becomes utterly self-contradictory to make the triumph of one's own viewpoint rather than the truth—a truth which is neither "mine" nor "thine"—the aim of discourse. This is not to say that true conversation does not require responsibility toward each other by the partners in the dialogue. But the chances of securing this are strengthened by a prior commitment to, or personal engagement with, the truth of the matter under discussion. According to Gadamer, fulfillment of the personal and interpersonal goals of the conversation hangs upon the realization of the transpersonal (and, hence, more consistently inter-personal) aims of gaining a common perspective and working out a common language as the elaboration of a common world of meaning (1965:

350, 422; 1975:331, 404). This pursuit, this search, is what saves the partners from manipulativeness as well as from extremes of trivialization and fanaticism.

Gadamer emphasizes that a key ploy of Socrates is to make the other's opinion stronger in relation to the perspective of the subject matter under discussion (1965:349; 1975:330). In the hard-edged dialectic, then, the true master of argument (as opposed to the mere debater) is actually the one unconcerned enough with arguing his opponent down to be capable of being the servant of the issue that moves in and through but remains irreducible to the subjective viewpoints of the parties to the discussion (1965:422; 1975: 404). Dialectic breaks through what Whitehead has called "the assumptions which appear so obvious that people do not know that they are assuming them, because no other way of putting things has ever occurred to them" (1965:348; 1975:329). It requires climbing behind one's own entrenched personality and, in Eliot's phrase, "all the trifling differences that are [one's] distinction." And so the efficacy of the Socratic-Platonic "art of questioning" (1965:346; 1975:327) depends on the surrender of oneself to a common action, a common entanglement in a common issue that alone makes a real exchange, a real contribution possible. Dialectic would realize in conversation that unique presence and authentic human weight that keeps it from becoming "discourse (as Wittgenstein said of high table conversation) that comes neither from the heart nor from the head" (Hough).

The dialectic art of questioning is promoted by the intention of truth already spontaneously operative in one's living, even though it may have hitherto been so eclipsed socially and culturally, so deflected by other desires and interests, as to be prevented from attaining a sufficiently directive and critical role. Remember, though, that the truth-<u>intention</u> is not already knowledge (1965:347; 1975:328); and it is satisfied only when truth is attained. Underlying Gadamer's warning that since the dialectical art tries to establish the real primacy of the truth-intention in actual conversation, it cannot be likened to a pure craft like carpentry (1965:347; 1975:330), is the fact that the craftsmen know fairly well exactly what the finished product will be like when they begin a "piece of work." But the true dialectician's distinction is the awareness that one does <u>not</u> know the outcome of the diverse lines of thinking that may unfold in the course of a discussion.

Plato and Aristotle stress that unlike Sophist eristic, dialectic singles out the truth-intention as the highest and most proper of human finalities. It is what pushes the knowing and willing subject beyond itself: it is an immanent principle of self-transcendence. The project of self-transcendence, however, is not to be understood 'existentialistically' as an arbitrary choice on the part of the subjective will, but as a primordial attunement or orientation. Getting a real apprehension of this sort of orientation would need not only a rehabilitation of the Greek notion of ethos (as of that in which an individual or a people abides, dwells, lives); but an explicit awareness that the human mind is capable of growth through its own self-directed effort (Phaedo, 90-91). Hence, dialectic operates by bringing the known-unknown goal of human aspiration to bear in discriminating and steering amidst what people commonly hold, think, and say (doxa), because doxic beauty and goodness (to kalon) often enough does not coincide with the good (to agathon) (Gadamer, 1978). Discrimination is both needed and meaningful because, on account of our inbuilt truth-intention, human beings are oriented in their speech and action not only on a biological scale of need-satisfactions (although this is also a possible and sometimes factual way of being oriented), but on a normative scale of truth-falsity and right-wrong. By asking questions about common opinions and in this way putting them to the test, dialectic lays bare the noble and ignoble things to which the partners in the dialogue are already committed; it suggests and sometimes even elicits conversion. Socratic conversion (periagoge) implies agreement with oneself; and Socratic-Platonic dialectic specifies that agreement-with-self normatively as exacting agreement with what is 'beyond' the self: reality (Voegelin, 1957, 1974, 1981).

Dialectic plays midwife to this self-transcending, transpersonal impulse at the core of the truth intention. As Burrell has put it:

> The question why pushes out to demand a framework within which even the studied opinion of an expert can be assessed. It is no respecter of persons; rather, it seeks for a ground which can be shared in common but does not require the support of anyone—expert or group—for it can establish itself (110).

The art of questioning is out after a true understanding of the matters broached, where "true" has an express note of transsubjective absoluteness and publicity. Correlatively, sustained inquiry reveals to the conversation-partners how they have fallen short of the potentialities in themselves that would more adequately correspond to the subject matter of the dispute as well as how—by questioning further—they might transcend themselves to a more adequate (more intelligent, more responsible) participation in the real. Hence, Gadamer's claim that in the process of posing questions about the matter at issue in a conversation there is a sense in which the subject matter puts the questioners into question is not just metaphorical. For Gadamer, the constitutive moment of genuine conversation is the occurrence of the openness signalled by this event.

This is why dialectic, then, so well exhibits the game-play (Spiel) structure of conversation (Gadamer, 1967:98-99). All the elements are there: the mediation of one's immediacy via 'ecstatic' participation in a transpersonal reality moving in and through the individual sharers; the medial structure in which 'activity' is, to use the medieval expression, a <u>pati</u>; the chance for self-realization in self-transcendence. Perhaps it is becoming clear why Gadamer uses the stringent nexus manifest in Socratic-Platonic dialectic between subject matter moving-in-and-through conversation and questioning/being-put-into question—with all the connotations of detachment and discipline which fidelity to that nexus in the dialectical process requires--to elucidate language-as-horizon.

C. Hermeneutic Experience as Conversation:
   Words as Correlatives of Questions

Now I would like to dwell on the component of questioning in Gadamer's conception of conversation. It is what most distinguishes his view of language as horizon from those of Heidegger and Rorty. According to Gadamer, questioning at once <u>supervenes</u> on experience and <u>lets</u> experience <u>become realized</u>. It supervenes on experience inasmuch as it arises out of and expresses immediacy in two distinct senses of immediacy: first, in the sense that questioning is provoked by and is about what is immediate <u>in intentione recta</u>: the data of sense and/or the (already mediated) immediacy of images, symbols, words, frameworks; secondly, in the sense that questioning itself is a unique expression of a <u>primordial wonder</u> (in whatever stage of historical differentiation it may have attained) that is immediate <u>in intentione obliqua</u>. Hence, questioning mediates immediacy in both senses; and so it is the mediation <u>par excellence</u>. Whereas picture-thinking of the nominalist prejudgment or the horizon of <u>Vorhandenheit</u> either eliminates mediation entirely or admits only the mediation of immediacy as it occurs <u>in intentione recta</u>, questioning is a mediation of immediacy which occurs <u>in intentione obliqua</u> as well. By bringing questioning to light in this way, Gadamer acknowledges the way in which the effective condition of actuality of the mediation of immediacy <u>in intentione recta</u> (1965:442; 1975:423-424) is always concomitant with the mediation of immediacy <u>in intentione obliqua</u>—that is, as he has expressed it: "the pivoting ... that happens to thinking as a turn-about irreducible to the conceptual order" (1965:443; 1975: 425), the shift in "the horizon that enclosed us up to that point" (1965:460; 1972:442).

For Gadamer, then, the act of questioning lets experience become realized because its occurrence sets experience within the unrestricted range of possible inquiry. In so doing, it expands the subject's scope of intending from the private world of internal and external immediacy to the universe of being.

This is what lets Gadamer call linguistic performance <u>speculative</u>: for "as the performance of meaning, as the event of genuine discourse, mutual comprehension, and understanding ... the finite possibilities of the word have been correlated with the intended meaning as to a direction heading off into the infinite" (1965:444; 1975:426). Unless I am mistaken, according to Gadamer, what safeguards meaning from becoming a <u>closed</u> totality while not completely forsaking all definition is precisely conscious intentionality <u>as questioning</u>. And so it is questioning that makes possible what takes place in authentic speech (<u>Sagen</u>) and mutual comprehension (<u>V</u>erstaendigung): a "hold[ing] ... what is said together with an infinitude of what is not said in the unity of a meaning, and so letting it be understood." In contrast, picture-thinking will be satisfied with and so strives for a "picturing of a fixed given (<u>Abbildung des fix Gegebenen</u>)" (1965:450; cf. also 445-46, 1975:431; also 426-428, 430-431). But those who have entered a dialectic of question and answer and actually begun to respond to its exactions (1965:446-447; 1975:428-429) "conduct themselves speculatively when their words do not picture some entity, but instead utter and allow to come to language a relationship to the totality of being" (1965:445, cf. also 446, 449; 1975:426-430). In short, Gadamer's conception of language as horizon points to a central fact: "Meaning is exactly the sense of direction or orientation (<u>Richtungssinn</u>) of a possible question" (1965:346; 1975:327).

Questioning or inquiry is not manipulative, because when it is authentic (<u>really</u> occurs) it is not, as it necessarily becomes within the horizon of picture-thinking, an abusive thing that imposes in advance whatever it wants to find. Rather it is what P. Ricoeur has called a "second naivete": an attentive listening. Gadamer speaks of the role of wonder in terms which make it clear that the peculiarity of the act of questioning is not that of a will-to-power that renders everything questionable at once, but of a will somewhat akin to a disciplining or asceticism whereby the questioner is simultaneously called into question:

> Thus every exertion of the desire to understand begins at the point when something one encounters strikes one as alien, challenging, disorientating. The Greeks had a very beautiful word for that whereby our understanding is jolted to a standstill; they called it the <u>atopon</u>. This really means: the place-less, that which is not to be brought under the schematisms of our intelligent expectations, and which therefore leaves us startled. The renowned Platonic doctrine that philosophizing begins with wonder means this becoming startled, this not getting any further on the basis of the preschematized expectations of our world-orientation, which calls us to take thought ... This being startled is so relative and so much related to knowledge and a deeper penetrating into the subject matter. Evidently the whole point of all this being startled and wonder and not getting anywhere in understanding is always coming further, knowing more discerningly (1970:365).

Hence real questioning is the opposite of a stubborn will toward closure and logical transparency. Such a will is a distortion imported by picture-thinking. Yes, questioning does seek intelligibility. But the genuine actuation of its quest ever incorporates this determinate, negative moment whose very integration in a new and better answer will always generate still another question with its determinate, negative moment (1965:423, 1975:405). "Questioning can have nothing to do with rehearsing, potential behavior, because questioning is not positing but a genuine trying out of possibilities in the sense of giving them a chance" (1965:357; 1975:338). Indeed by acknowledging the dynamic and unrestricted character of questioning we realize that the intelligibility which can fully satisfy it can not be identified with any totalizing image of the universe or englobing system (Weltbild); it can be compatible, neither with a forgetfulness of mystery nor with eliminating all the mystery from the field of the meaningful. Not at all. As Gadamer expressed it:

> One has no genuine experiences without the activity of questioning. The knowledge that the subject matter is otherwise and not the way one first thought obviously presupposes the passage through the question as to whether the thing is this way or that. The openness lying within the essence of experience is, logically considered, precisely this openness of this way (So) or that (So). It has the structure of the question. And just as the dialectical negativity of experience found its perfection in the idea of a realized experience in which we "enter into" our finitude and limitedness as a whole, so also the question finds its realization in a radical negativity: the knowledge of one's not knowing. It is the famed Socratic 'docta ignorantia' that in the most extreme negativity of the aporia the true superiority of questioning opens up (1965:344-345; 1975:325-326).

This central recognition of the significance of questioning on Gadamer's part sets the stage for a theoretical apprehension of the work that is free from the illusions of the nominalist prejudgment and the horizon of Vorhandenheit. It liberates it decisively from Descartes' ego cogito, from Kant's Verstand, from Hegel's absolutes Wissen. It places it rather in the vicinity of the rarely noticed sources of human being and knowing only hinted at by Kant's earlier treatment of Einbildungskraft. For questioning is the chief condition to be fulfilled in order for word (a) to proceed from the spirit as both immediate and for the spirit; and (b) to refer to what is other than the spirit (namely, the subject matter intended in questioning) not as to "a pregiven thing having nothing whatsoever to do with word (sprachlos Vorgegebenes)" but as to something that "receives in the word its own proper determinacy" (1965:450; 1975:431-432). As Gadamer has explained it: "The emergence of a question as it were breaks up the being of what is questioned. The logos that unfolds this broken-up being is therefore ever already an answer. It itself has meaning in the direction (Sinne) of the question" (1965:345; 1975:326).

When the word is located in terms of the operative horizon of one's questioning, it becomes manifest, according to Gadamer, that "language is language exactly at the point when it is pure actus exercitus, i.e., when it goes about making visible what is being said and as it were vanishes itself" (1967:146). Gadamer thematizes this sort of awareness of language as a speculative identity. From such identity it follows that:

> The existence of agreement about things that is actuated in language bespeaks as such neither a primacy of the thing nor a primacy of the human mind that makes use of a linguistic instrument of agreement. Rather the correspondence that finds its concretion in linguistic world-experience is as such the absolutely (schlechthinnige) prior (1967:67).

I take this to mean that the coming to presence of things in word and as worded is experienced as such only when the horizon of meaning actually corresponds to the horizon of questioning.

> There exists no statement which one can apprehend solely with respect to the content which it lays out, if one wishes to grasp it in its truth. Every statement is motivated. Every statement has presuppositions which it does not articulate. Only one who thinks these presuppositions as well can really measure the truth of a statement. Now I claim: the ultimate logical form of such motivation of every statement is the question. Not the judgmental proposition but the question has the primacy in logic ... the primacy of the question as opposed to the statement means, however, that the statement is essentially answer ... Hence there is no understanding of any statement which does not gain from an understanding of the question to which it responds its sole criterion (1967:354).

In the light of this correspondence one can apprehend with Gadamer that what is essential is not just that human knowledge of any subject matter whatsoever happens to be bound up with language; but that all human language-in-use contains a reference to some subject matter (1965:417, also 423; 1975:401-402, 405).

Hence the correspondence (Entsprechung) defined by Gadamer as absolutely prior has nothing to do with picture-thinking or with Rorty's "mirror of nature." As such it removes the conventional moment of language-in-use from either the realm of arbitrary decisions of some linguistic community or from some supposedly non-arbitrary basic framework describing the primordial core of human experience to which all other frameworks are reduced either logically or epistemologically. Language-in-use is located instead within the non-picturable and normative compass of the horizon of possible inquiry (1967:67; 1965:408; 1975:391).

The role of questioning which highlights word-experience in its horizonal implications also sets aside the usual and dominant instrumental theories of the word. For it dispels any idea that the intending or act of meaning which proceeds from questioning may be adequately described either in terms of following a blueprint in order to produce some object or of the conceptualist assumption that we know by what we unconsciously produce rather than by what we are in our intelligence and reasonableness (Lonergan). To specify the difference between, on the one hand, making as plan-following or understanding as reading off concepts, and on the other, the unique sort of causality actually involved in the act of meaning, we recall Gadamer's emphasis that thinking is essentially a matter of asking ever further questions; and so the word pertains to thinking, as Gadamer commenting on Aquinas says, not as exteriorization (Aeusserung, for example, vocalization, as the Stoic verbum prolatum) but as its perfection, "which is reached as it were in this self-utterance" (that is, inner word [1965:339; 1975:382]); this inner word proceeds from understanding as Aquinas formulated it, ut actus ex actu, so that (as Gadamer has put it) "the word is not first formed after knowledge is finished, ... but it is the performance-actuation (Vollzug) of knowledge itself (1965:400-401, 410-411; 1975: 383, 392-393); and the word comes to presence as the perfection of thinking in speculative identity with the subject matter (1965:402, 1975:384-385). Precisely because of questioning as originative horizon of word, word (or language-in-use) as consciously proceeding as answer may not be compared with a product in the ordinary sense or with anything at one's disposal like instruments or goods for consumption. Far from being the lord and master imposing his dominion over one's world, the questioning person is, in Gadamer's words, "bound to language which is not only the language of the one speaking [gen. subj. FL], but also of the conversation which things hold with us" (1967:147;1965:450-452, 440-441; 1975:432-434, 423-425). As embedded in the movement of questioning, language itself becomes operative not as tool or product but as horizon with "an immediate relationship to the infinity of beings" (1965:429; 1975:411).

> Each word breaks forth from a center and has reference to a totality by which alone it is a word. Each word lets both the totality of the language to which it belongs sound out and the totality of the world-perspective in which it is enrooted appear. Therefore, even as the happening of its own particular moment, each word lets the unspoken to which it is related as answering and hinting be present as well (1965:434; 1975:415-416).

Now the realization that word or language-in-use functions as horizon also means that reflection is not to be equated with the deformed image of reflection entertained by the horizon of Vorhandenheit. Word as horizonal (that is, the concrete way word is at work as response) means that in the act of referring to something explicitly (in intentione recta, in actu signato) the process of working is at the same time self-reflective (in intentione obliqua, in actu exercito):

> Through Husserl (in his doctrine of anonymous intentionalities), and through Heidegger (in the demonstration of the ontological foreshortening which lurks in Idealism's concepts of subject and object) we have learned to see through the false objectifying (Vergegenstaendlichung) which weighs down the notion of reflection. There quite certainly does exist an inner turning back of intentionality that in no

wise raises what is thus cointended to the status of thematic object. Brentano (in taking up Aristotelian insights) had already seen this. I would not know how one might want to conceive the enigmatic form of being of language at all if not by departing from this insight. One has to distinguish the 'effective' reflection (to use the words of J. Lohmann) from the explicit and thematic reflection which has evolved in Western linguistic history and which, inasmuch as it makes everything object, has, as science, fashioned the presuppositions of the planetary civilization of tomorrow (1967:125).

Word as correlative with the horizon of questioning does not reveal one's personal a priori to be what it has been for all the more sophisticated picture-thinkers: a categorical structure or a logical form which is assumed to render knowing possible (i.e., a blueprint of all blueprints, a kind of meta-tableau or -picture). On account of the negativity built into questioning it is unable to be domesticated by technique or identified with some conceptual scheme as a timeless and unchanging norm. Positively speaking, Gadamer's a priori amounts to no more or less than "a self-correcting process which formulates, refines, and criticizes frameworks in its own light."

Language as horizon brings to light a contrast between those like Aquinas and, I think, Gadamer for which the differentia of human presence-to-world is an "apriorism of the lumen intellectuale, the potens (n.b.) omnia facere et fieri proper to a created participation in uncreated light on the one hand; and those like Rorty and probably Heidegger, who interpret this differentia in terms of picture-thinking, on the other.

This is the source of the radical division between the 'method' operative within the horizon of the nominalist prejudgment as crystallized by Descartes and that "discipline of questioning and inquiry which constitutes a seeking of the truth" which is played out in Gadamer's polemic in Wahrheit und Methode.

Do we conceive of the normative horizon of human existence in terms of a series of principles, axioms, and rules for the purpose of controlling, mastering, dominating being (Gadamer, 1967:22-26, 50, 107-108)? Or do we conceive of it in terms of the immanent normativeness of a conscious intentionality which by asking questions ever goes beyond every finite and determined totality in an attempt to correspond with being (1967:69) in the sense of what Gadamer calls a primordial Zugehoerigkeit (1965:434; cf. 434-441; 1975:416-423) or affinity? When one finds with Aquinas and Gadamer and Lonergan that only the second alternative manifests phenomenological accuracy and adequacy, one is not al all thereby forced to claim--as Augustine, Descartes, Kant, Hegel, and Husserl seem to have thought necessary—that this implies a non-verifiable, simple identify of the ultimate ground of human knowing (God) with the immanent reason why man knows (1965:432-433, 461; 1975:414-415; 442-443). For finite presence-to-self-in-world-as-worded is rooted primordially not in a sovereign knowledge of everything about everything (nor even in the basic blueprint [for example, Leibniz's mathesis universalis, Descartes' Regulae, Wittgenstein's "logical form"]); but in its immanent capacity for "undiverted listening" (unbeirrtes Hoerens), which is actuated in the exertion (Anstrengung) of "being negative toward oneself," within the conversation which reality holds with the finite human subject (1965:441; 1975:422).

NOTE

/1/ All of the citations of Gadamer's Wahrheit und Methode are taken from the second edition of that work in German. I have used my own translations, but have provided references to the corresponding texts in the English translation, Truth and Method (New York: The Seabury Press, 1975).

WORKS CONSULTED

Burrell, David B.
1971 "What the Dialogues Show about Inquiry." The Philosophical Forum 3:104-125.

Gadamer, Hans-Georg
1965 Wahrheit und Methode. Grundzuege einer philosophischen Hermeneutik. Mohr (Paul Siebeck). Second edition; first eidtion 1960.

1967 Kleine Schriften I: Philosophie. Hermeneutik. Tuebingen: Mohr (Paul Siebeck).

1970 "Sprache und Verstehen." Zeitwende 6:364-377.

1975 Truth and Method. Trans. edited by G. Barden and J. Cumming. New York: Seabury.

1977 Philosophische Lehrjahre. Eine Rueckschau. Frankfurt: V. Klostermann.

1978 Die Idee des Guten zwischen Plato und Aristoteles. Heidelberg: Carl Winter, Universitaetsverlag.

1981a "What Is Practice? The Conditions of Social Reason." In Reason in the Age of Science. Trans. F.G. Lawrence. Cambridge, MA: MIT Press, 69-87.

1981b "Hermeneutics as Practical Philosophy." In Reason in the Age of Science, 88-112.

1981c "Hermeneutics as a Theoretical and Practical Task." In Reason in the Age of Science, 113-138.

Lawrence, Frederick G.
1981 "Translator's Introduction." In Reason in the Age of Science, by H.-G. Gadamer, ix-xxxiii.

Lonergan, Bernard
1967 Verbum: Word and Idea in Aquinas. Ed. David Burrell. Notre Dame, IN: Notre Dame University.

Rorty, Richard
1979 Philosophy and the Mirror of Nature. Princeton, NJ: Princeton University Press.

1982 "The Fate of Philosophy." The New Republic, October 18: 28-34.

Sala, Giovanni B.
1971 Das Apriori in der menschlichen Erkenntnis: Eine Studie ueber Kants Kritik der reinen Vernunft und Lonergans Insight. Meisenheim am Glan: Hain.

1974 "L'Origine del Concetto. Un Problema Kantiano e una Riposta Tomista." Revista di Filosofia neo-scolastica 66:975-1017.

Voegelin, Eric
1974   "Reason: The Classic Experience." <u>The Southern Review</u> 10:237-264.

1981   "Wisdom and the Magic of the Extreme: A Meditation." <u>The Southern Review</u> 17:235-287.

1957   <u>Plato and Aristotle (Order and History</u> III). Baton Rouge: Louisiana State University.

CONSCIOUSNESS AND ORDER
FOREWORD TO 'ANAMNESIS' (1966)

Eric Voegelin
Stanford University

[The 'Vorwort' to Anamnesis: Zur Theorie der Geschichte und Politik (Munich, 1966), has been been translated by the author himself. Anamnesis marks the pivot of the movement of Voegelin's thought from the first three volumes of Order and History (1956-1957) to the fourth, The Ecumenic Age (1974). The concentration on a philosophy of consciousness announced by the 'Foreword' continues in Voegelin's work on the forthcoming fifth volume. A whole series of other studies, which followed Anamnesis, have carried on the program of this 'Foreword' /1/. The English translation of Anamnesis (Notre Dame, 1978) replaced the 'Foreword' with a new essay, "Remembrance of Things Past," and omitted a number of the special studies, most of which were already available, in some form, in English /2/.]

The problems of human order in society and history originate in the order of consciousness. Hence the philosophy of consciousness is the centerpiece of a philosophy of politics.

That the poor state of political science--through its being mired in neo-Kantian theories of knowledge, value-relating methods, historicism, descriptive institutionalism, and ideological speculations on history--could be overcome only by a new philosophy of consciousness, was clear to me already in the twenties. The first encounter with the most important theories of consciousness that were known to me at the time is to be found in my book Ueber die Form des Amerikanischen Geistes (1928), especially in the chapter on "Zeit und Existenz." The critical results of this first attempt are still valid; but at the time there was wanting the philosophical and historical knowledge that would have enabled me to move substantially beyond mere criticism. Ever since that time the efforts to arrive at clarity about a theory of consciousness have never ceased; they were continued through the decades in variegated work on phenomena of order and the reduction of the phenomena of order to the logos of consciousness. The most important result of these efforts was the insight that a "theory" of consciousness in the sense of generically valid propositions concerning a pre-given structure was impossible. For consciousness is not a given to be deduced from outside but an experience of participation in the ground of being whose logos has to be brought to clarity through the meditative exegesis of itself. The illusion of a "theory" had to give way to the reality of the meditative process; and this process had to go through its phases of increasing experience and insight.

The character of consciousness as a process of augmenting insight into its own logos determines the form of the volume [Anamnesis] herewith presented.

Above all the volume relates the principal phases of the meditative process: from the first decisive insight into its problem (Part I) to its provisionally last formulation (Part III). The studies which articulate the critical breakthrough were written in 1943; they stem from the correspondence with Alfred Schuetz and have hitherto not been published. Part I of the volume brings them under the title Remembrance and lets them be preceded by the "In Memoriam Alfred Schuetz." The insights of these studies became the precondition for the development of a theory of politics in The New Science of Politics (1952) and Order and History (1956-57). As to the provisionally last phase of the meditation, I had to deliver, in June 1965, a lecture on the question "What is Political Reality?" The subsequent thinking through of the problems let it grow to three or four times its original size; and the not foreseen result was a comprehensive and momentarily satisfactory new formulation of a philosophy of consciousness. Part III of this volume presents the enlarged study under the title The Order of Consciousness.

Consciousness is the luminous center radiating the concrete order of human existence into society and history. A philosophy of politics is empirical—in the pregnant sense of an inquiry into the experiences which penetrate the whole area of reality that we express by the symbol "man" with their order. The work of this philosophy requires, as we said, the constant exchange between studies on concrete cases of order and analyses of consciousness which make the human order in society and history intelligible. Since the analyses of consciousness presuppose the historical phenomena of order (and refer to them only as exemplars), a series of special studies was placed between Parts I and III. These special studies are supposed to show how the analyses of consciousness arise from the work on the historical materials. The studies were selected so that (a) larger complexes of materials would become visible which require a philosophy of consciousness for their theoretical penetration and so that (b) they will demonstrate by their analytical work on the materials how a philosophy of conciousness develops empirically. The special studies want to stress the close empirical correlation between the analysis of consciousness and the phenomena of order. As the consciousness is the center that radiates the concrete order of human existence into society and history, so the empiricism of social and historical phenomena of order reaches into the empiricism of consciousness and its experiences of participation.

A few remarks on specific correlations:

The first of the special studies treats the problem of Historiogenesis, i.e. the phenomenon of linear constructions of history in the empires of the ancient Orient. The conventional assumption that the cultures of the ancient Orient had an idea only of "cyclical time" proved to be wrong. The ancient cultures have in fact produced the symbolism of linear history, and they have characteristically produced them in the context of severe disturbances of political order. Linear constructions arise from the fears for preservation and legitimacy of order; they have the function to restore or to legitimate the respective order, or to establish it by revolution. Moreover, the violent distortions of historical materials for this purpose are as characteristic for the constructions of the ancient Orient as for the modern philosophies of history. The equivalence of politically obsessive constructions in the media of mythical and ideological speculation is brought to attention by this analysis. — This first study is balanced by the last one, on "Eternal Being in Time" (1964). While the first one is concerned with the symbolism of linear time the last one explores the problem of the "flowing presence" in which time and eternity meet. It opens the perspective of a philosophy of history beyond the obsessional constructions and, for this purpose, intimates essential problems in a philosophy of consciousness, such as the theory of "language indices" that is resumed in Part III of the present volume.

A second complex of problems is circumscribed by studies on classical politics (1963). The paper on "The Right by Nature" traces the topical symbolism of Natural Law to its philosopher's origin in the Aristotelian inquiries into the right order of society and its origin in the existentially right order. The study on the question "What is Nature?" complements the preceding one, for the problem of a "Right by Nature" requires clarity on the "Nature" that is supposed to legitimate the "Right." In this context there appear the Aristotelian problems of a consciousness of the ground which are further elaborated in Part III of the volume.

The third complex concerns the relations between Western civilization and the Mongol empires. On the occasion of studies on Renaissance politics, I noticed that the appearance of Timur moved the humanistic thinkers to develop a new myth of power-political and historic-epochal action. The development of the myth reaches into the very conception of Machiavelli's Prince. From the occupation with this problem arose the monograph on "The Timur-Image of the Humanists" (1937). In the course of the subsequent studies on the relations between the West and the Mongol empires I encountered the Orders of Submission issued by the Mongol khans to the Western powers. Submitted to critical classification and edition, the documents proved to be sources of high importance, not only for the Mongol constructions of a right to conquer the world but for the understanding of ecumenical empire-building in general. The results were originally published under the title "The Mongol Orders of Submission to European Powers, 1245-1255." For the present publication, under the title "The Order of God," the analytical parts were elaborated so that the parallels with the modern empire-law of Communist world conquest would become more manifest. With the two monographs here presented began the further explorations of the problem of empire-building which, however, have not yet come to their conclusion. Intimations of a theory of empire, that up to now has been neglected in political science in favor of the theory of the national state, are to be found in "Historiogenesis" and in "Eternal Being in Time," as well as in Part III. A first survey of its main problems is given in my London lecture, "World Empire and the Unity of Mankind" (1962).

The fourth complex is formed by two studies concerning the areas of ideologies. "Bakunin's Confession" (1946) further elaborates the theory of empire for the case of a revolutionary imperial dreamer. The lecture on John Stuart Mill, "On Readiness to Rational Discussion" (1959), treats the decay of the freedom of discussion through the refusal to discuss rationally as well as the techniques of preventing discussions. It connects the studies on classical politics with the analysis of consciousness in Part III.

A philosophy of order is the process through which we find the order of our existence as human beings in the order of consciousness. Plato has let this philosophy be dominated by the symbol of "Anamnesis," Remembrance. Remembered, however, will be what has been forgotten; and we remember the forgotten—sometimes with considerable travail—because it should not remain forgotten. The culpably forgotten will be brought to the presence of knowledge through remembrance and in the tension to knowledge oblivion reveals itself as the state of non-knowledge, of the agnoia of the soul in the Platonic sense. Knowledge and non-knowledge are states of existential order and disorder. What has been forgotten, however, can be remembered only because it is a knowledge in the mode of oblivion which through its presence in oblivion arouses the existential unrest that will urge toward its raising into the mode of knowledge. Oblivion and knowledge are modes of consciousness of which the first can be raised into the second through remembrance. Remembering is the activity of consciousness by which the forgotten, i.e. the latent knowledge in consciousness, is raised from unconsciousness into the presence of consciousness. In the Enneads (IV,3,30) Plotinus has described this action as the transition from nonarticulate thinking to articulate thinking that perceives itself. Through an act of perceiving attention (antilepsis), the non-articulated knowledge (noema) is transformed into conscious knowledge; and this antileptic knowledge then becomes fixed through language (logos). Remembrance thus, is the process by which non-articulated (ameres) knowledge can be raised into the realm of language-images (to phantistikon) so that, through expression in the pregnant sense of becoming a thing in the external world (eis to exo), it will become linguistically articulated presence in consciousness.

In my Order and History I have analyzed how Plato's insight into remembrance changes, and gains in depth, from the early to the late dialogues: (a) In the Meno, the popular myth of a pre-existence of the soul is introduced in order to make intelligible how the knowledge concerning the eidos of virtue can be raised from worldly oblivion through philosophical action to a present of consciousness that will correspond to its full knowledge in pre-existence. (b) In the Republic, the tradition of the myth changes to the form of philosophical mythopoesis; the knowledge concerning the order of man and society that originates in the ordering of the soul through the vision of the Agathon is now understood in its tension to oblivion in the Cave of the world with its shadow-plays of order, i.e. to the existential disorder of the polis; the representative of the knowledge of order now becomes the philosopher-king of the Kallipolis and the royal philosopher Socrates-Plato creates the philosophical myth of Judgment. (c) In Timaeus-Critias, finally, remembrance raises the comprehending knowledge of human-social existence attuned to the order of history and the cosmos from the unconscious into consciousness. The remembrance expands into a philosophy of consciousness in its tensions of conscious and unconscious, of latency and presence of knowledge, of knowing and forgetting, of order and disorder in personal, social and historical existence, as well as to a philosophy of symbols in which these tensions find their linguistic expression. However, the knowledge of man concerning his tension to the divine ground of being remains the center of consciousness; what is remembered is the origins, the beginnings, and the grounds of order in the present existence of man. The accents placed by Plotinus on the linguistic articulation of remembering consciousness bring to attention that in relation to the flowing presence of consciousness, in the tension between time and eternity in the Platonic Metaxy, all symbolic expression is a shape in the externality of the world and its time. When remembrance reaches articulation in the linguistic expression of knowledge it falls to the conditions of the world; in the external world the symbol can separate from remembering consciousness, it can become opaque for the experience expressed; and the remembering knowledge can again sink from the presence of consciousness into the latency of oblivion. In times of social disorder, like our present time, we are surrounded by the detritus of symbols expressing past remembrance, as well as by the symbols of revolt against the state of oblivion; hence the work of remembrance must be started again.

The anamnetic character of the analysis collected in the present volume determined its title.

NOTES

/1/ These studies include the following:

1967	"Immortality: Experience and Symbol." <u>Harvard Theological Review</u> 60:235-279.
1969	"History and Gnosis." In <u>The Old Testament and Christian Faith</u>. Ed. by B. Anderson. New York: Herder & Herder, 64-89.
1970	"Equivalences of Experience and Symbolization in History." In <u>Eternita e Storia</u> (Florence). Reprint. <u>Philosophical Studies</u> (The National University of Ireland) 28 (1981):88-103.
1970	"The Eclipse of Reality." In <u>Phenomenology and Social Reality</u>. Ed. by M. Natanson. The Hague: M. Nijhoff, 1985-194.
1971	"The Turn of the Screw." <u>The Southern Review</u> 7:3-67.
1971	"The Gospel and Culture." In <u>Jesus and Man's Hope</u>, vol. 2. Ed. by D.G. Miller and D.Y. Hadidian. Pittsburgh: Pittsburgh Theological Seminary, 59-101.
1971	"On Hegel--A Study in Sorcery." <u>Studium Generale</u> 24:335-368. Reprint. <u>The Study of Time</u>. Ed. by J.T. Fraser. Springer Verlag, 1972, 418-451.
1974	"Reason: The Classic Experience." <u>The Southern Review</u> 10:237-264. Reprint. <u>Anamnesis</u>. By Eric Voegelin. University of Notre Dame Press, 1978, 89-115.
1975	"Response to Professor Altizer." <u>Journal of the American Academy of Religion</u> 43:765-772.
1981	"Wisdom and the Magic of the Extreme: A Meditation." <u>Eranos Jahrbuch</u> 46:341-409; <u>The Southern Review</u> 17:235-287.
1981	"Der meditative Ursprung philosophischen Ordnungswissens." <u>Zeitschrift fuer Politik</u> 28:131-137. Translated by F.G. Lawrence in the present volume.

/2/ For the reader's convenience, some of these essays are listed here, including the one on "World Empire" referred to in the 'Foreword' but not included in the English translation of <u>Anamnesis</u>.

1937	"Das Timurbild der Humanisten: Eine Studie zur politischen Mythenbildung." <u>Zeitschrift fuer Oeffentliches Recht</u> (Vienna) 17:515-582.
1941	"The Mongol Orders of Submission to European Powers, 1245-1255." <u>Byzantion</u> 15:378-413.
1946	"Bakunin's Confession." <u>Journal of Politics</u> 8:24-43.

1961   "On Readiness to Rational Discussion." In Freedom and Serfdom. Ed. by A. Hunold. Reidel Publishing Company, 269-284.

1962   "World Empire and the Unity of Mankind." International Affairs 38:170-183.

n.d.   "Historiogenesis." Expanded into chapter one of The Ecumenic Age (Order and History 4), 59-113.

THE MEDITATIVE ORIGIN
OF THE PHILOSOPHICAL KNOWLEDGE OF ORDER

Eric Voegelin
Stanford University

[This essay, a transcription of a lecture given by Dr. Voegelin at a symposium entitled "Politische Philosophie heute," appeared as "Der meditative Ursprung philosophischen Ordnungwissens" in Zeitschrift fuer Politik 28 (1981):130-137. With Dr. Voegelin's kind permission, it has been translated by Frederick G. Lawrence.]

An investigation of the meditative origin of the philosophical knowledge of order has to set out from the situation in which we live and from which the problem of truth first becomes a problem. From what source do we know that what we have available to us is not the truth? And how do we attain this insight, if we do not already realize what the truth is for which we first have to search? From the outset, therefore, we find ourselves in an existential tension that consists in the fact that we observe phenomena of untruth and problems of disorder in our environment, and on the basis of such observations we seek to discover an order about which we realize in anticipation that something akin to it exists, but it first has to be discovered. This tension of being moved, of questing and finding, is an initial instance of such meditative tension. For this reason, in the Greek origins of philosophical thought we have notions like zetesis (questing), kinesis (the condition of being moved to search), and nous (the medium of the soul in which this quest unravels). Hence from the very start we begin not with any definitions, but with movements, with spiritual tensions within which the human person in a concrete society lives. In every concrete society in which thought in this mode arises, such tensions are available more or less fundamentally, more or less efficaciously, although they may vary in particular cases. But the basic tension we call philosophy should always be understood in its primordial sense as love of wisdom, and not in the sense of Hegel, who in his Phenomenology of Spirit dismantles the love of wisdom in order to replace it with wisdom. Here the following problem becomes clear: First of all, there is present this tension which historically is precisely the philosophical tension. Secondly, here already we have a misconstruction of this tension which I call "egophanic." The misconstruction consists in eliminating the tension itself and wanting to transform it into a completely resolved possession of wisdom. You see, there is no question here of a Hegelian way of philosophizing; on the contrary, I would say that already by reason of his thesis of transforming love of wisdom, Hegel is not a philosophical thinker at all, but a magical constructor. So much then for a preliminary clarification of the situation within which we live. In any situation like this, meditative thought has to clear away the elements of disorder of its time in order to reattain a truth about reality. For this reason I have mentioned the element of disorder we find in Hegel. The same holds for Marx or Comte, both of whom formulated definitively valid doctrines. Definitively valid doctrines of this sort belong among the things that have to be swept away philosophically in the present situation as causes of public disorder.

Now you might say that it is quite am ambitious enterprise to believe oneself capable of sweeping away Hegelianism, Positivism, Marxism, and so forth. Of course, one cannot do so, but one can still call phenomena of disorder as such by name and argue against them in any society where these phenomena of disorder are socially dominant, as long as there is no totalitarian control present to prohibit doing so.

That is the situation in which we find ourselves. Permit me now to perform a bit of this job of cleaning up.

One of the grand constructions that has survived historically and which needs to be cleared away is of a theological nature. It is the theological distinction between natural reason and revelation, which goes back to the middle ages. In my view, there is no such thing as either natural reason or revelation. Instead, what we are dealing with here is a misconstruction, made in the interests of a theological systematization, of certain real entitative structures. They are to be designated more proximately as follows: On the one hand we have a so-called philosophical development that, prescinding from the fact that it is philosophical, is also an ethnic development; that is to say, an occurrence that took place within Hellenic culture. It is an ethnically Hellenic cultural event, which has to be understood in its connections, preconditions, and results. On the other hand, there is the so-called revelatory culture, which goes back to Israel and the movement of Judaism, which then had its culmination in Christ. Here we have an ethnically Israelite culture. Thus, we have to do with the categories of two ethnic cultures, each of which is concerned with the quest for truth, but in quite different forms. These distinguishable forms then get transmogrified into the form of the natural and that of the divinely revealed quest for the truth, for the purpose of letting the Judeo-Christian form dominate.

In terms of history, of course, the entire matter looks quite different. Within the overall history of the Hellenes, every Hellenic thinker since the time for which we have literary inscriptions, which is to say, since Hesiod, has been aware that whatever he has to say comes not from his natural reason, but from divine revelation; and further, that he lives out of

a tension of searching and receiving, that is, in a twofold movement of a
divine-human kind, which sets forth from the divine. Every Hellenic culture
from Hesiod to Plato and Aristotle is aware of this revelatory moment and also
speaks of it explicitly. The assertion that there is a matter of natural reason
here is a clumsy and unreliable falsification of the historical documents.

On the other side we have the problem of the Israelite-Christian
quest for truth, which once again is accentuated differently. If we wish to
establish the ethnic difference, then we shall find that among the Greeks the
accent always falls on the search, on the zetesis. Once a truth is discovered, then whatever was hitherto believed, for example, a mythically more
compact image of the gods, is relegated to the category of the pseudos (of
falsehood or lie). In the Israelite context, the matter looks otherwise. The
predecessors are not put down as liars or falsifiers, but as persons who had
also seen a truth already, but who now have to be interpreted anew as well.
Thus we have a scheme of reinterpretation--a more general phenomenon that
is to be observed not only in Israelite culture. For example, in Indian culture we have recourse to the Vedas; and this recourse has the consequence
that all further Hindu philosophy, to the degree that it too has distanced
itself from this original form, has to enter on the scene as interpretation of
the Vedas. Here contexts of interpretation are produced in which the old
truth is newly interpreted, even if this new truth no longer has very much
to do with old. This constantly comes up in cultures in which the awareness
of being divinely moved in the quest is especially emphasized. This phenomenon should have social causes. In Hellas we have the almost unique situation in which the spiritual order of the society is not represented by a
national or imperial priesthood. The priesthood of the Hellenes was local and
ritualistic, but not organized, as were the Egyptian or Israelite ones, along
doctrinaire, general cultural, national, or imperial lines. The compact mythical representations of the truth were enacted on the local level, so that in
this connection one can speak less of an ethnically Hellenic culture, than of
the local city cultures, which manifest certain common characteristics. If,
then, a movement of the sort made present by philosophy arises on this level
of local culture, it has a freer space to operate than in social contexts in
which a nationally or imperially organized priesthood has already established
what that truth is with which one enters into conflict when one proceeds to
propose a countertruth. This, therefore, was not the problem in Hellas.
Hence, in classical philosophy we find even a concrete instance, which might
not normally occur to us, in Aristotle's Metaphysics, Book Delta: simple
enumerations of meanings of terms, for example the term 'arche,' followed by
the enumeration of the meanings of the word 'aition,' which partially overlap.
Out of this listing of different meanings there is gradually elaborated then
what it is that terms like origin or ground and the like can possibly mean in

the meditative sense of the spiritual movement of the quest for wisdom. What is being elaborated from the very start, then, is a sort of scientific-philological presupposition.

This appears altogether different in the Israelite context: here a prophet has express recourse to forms of revelation with a Babylonian and Egyptian provenance. When a Jeremiah narrates his experience of revelation, he narrates it in a form that an Egyptian Pharoah would use to tell how he was preborn of God for his office and so on, and how he is therefore the Son of God, who has to speak out the truth. An imperial context of truth is present here, then, and not a scientific-philological investigation concerning the false use of terms which now have to be corrected. In a revelational context of the kind presented in the Israelite-Christian culture, there is always recourse to the divine spirit, the ruah, from which we get pneuma in the Greek translation. This spirit—which is the reason why I name the accent on revelation 'pneumatic'—ethnically determines the problem of a Christianity that grows out of the Jewish-Israelite contexts. Of course, the word pneuma comes up in the Greek context as well. Anaximenes has a pneuma theory very similar to that of the Book of Genesis; but in this case it is not a matter of a dominant theory. The dominant theory will be the noetic zetesis, the search.

We are dealing therefore with two different types of the quest for truth. Now when these two different ethnic cultures are brought into an imperial context, as occurred in the great ecumenic empires, there are mutual cultural influences; from this results the attempt to formulate a type of truth which somehow joins together the most successful of the different quests after truth that have taken place previously. This was the problem from which a Jewish theology arose for the first time with Philo, and then a Christian theology in marked dependency upon Philonic theology: a theology which unites revelational elements from the Israelite-Jewish context with the philosophical language which stems from the Hellenic context. So there emerges from the great events in cultural history such as the formation of the ecumenic empires a mixed culture in which one seeks to bring into equilibrium ethnic differences through a systematic doctrine of natural reason and pneumatic revelation. Such a systematic doctrine, which tries to bring revelation and natural reason into one construction, belongs among the things that have to be cleared away today. This has to happen neither on the basis of any anti-theological or anti-Christian animus, nor out of pro- or anti-philosophical grounds, but simply because we no longer need them. Today our historical knowledge is incomparably greater. We know the history of Israel and the history of Hellas; we can draw historical comparisons with India, Persia, and China; and we can name exactly the problems at stake. In the present ecumenic situation of science and scholarship it would not make sense to want to maintain this categorization—which does not mean that it perhaps should not be maintained in a theological context where it has exclusively to do with the problems of an ecclesiastical organization of a huge group of human beings; here a careful procedure is in order. But in a scholarly or scientific context one has to be clear about how such things have come about. In general such investigations do not disrupt the problem of truth which involves these kinds of insights in any way. The noetic formation among the Greeks is also not bothered by the fact that one understands what it is all about and knows the sources. It is matter of the quest for truth.

Thus the meditative problem here moves into the center of our attention. It can be accentuated from one side, that is to say, from the human side, as a questing. I would call this the noetic attitude. From the other side, the revelatory side one can accentuate the factor of movement. I would call this the pneumatic attitude. Both are present within the meditative problem. The tension arises between the being-moved from the divine side and the questing from the human side. The divine side and the human side, then, are presupposed in a process of questing and of being-moved. Such a symbolic framework as I have just used—a divine reality that moves, a concrete human being who quests, a process of questing and being-moved—such a framework I name a 'complex.' By the term 'complex' is to be understood that this process of movement and questing (which is explored here) should not be cut up into pieces or fragmentized in such a way that a study of human being—an anthropology, then—emerges from a concentration on the human side; or that a theology gets formulated from the confinement to the divine side. Also impermissible is the separation of the process in the form of a process philosophy that would examine only the process lying between the two poles and lead to a psychology. All three forms—'anthropology,' 'theology,' and 'psychology'—are types of deformation and impermissible in a meditative investigation. This would be a matter of hypostatizing poles existing in a tension. None of the elements in a process such as the one we are familiar with can be fragmentized and hypostatized. Thus you can see what a great practical significance our considerations have. All fragmentization into anthropologies, theologies, and psychologies is excluded. One has to deal with the processes that really take place, with meditative events. The analysis of the event may not be parcelled out into deforming fragmentations. Conversely, it will thereby once again be analysis of disorder of the age, since methodologies and schools which bring this about are mistaken and incompetent in the light of the historical information we have today. This problem of event will be a basic category, together with that of the complex which cannot be fragmentized, with which one has to work. Here a word out of the Platonic vocabulary has just come up, which I use in my own analysis:

the In-between. This reality is neither the human reality nor the divine reality, but what passes 'between' these realities, without this 'In-between's' having to be once again independently fragmentized or hypostatized. It is a question, therefore, neither of a psychology of the subject, nor only of an activity of God; it is always a matter of the response, of the movements and countermovements.

In this manner, however, we have located a problem that leads to further complexes. Until now I have spoken of the central meditative complex that has been elaborated by Plato and Aristotle; but from this there results a further problem. It is clear that what since the seventeenth century has been called the subject-object tension is incompatible with this interpretation. Permit me to draw attention to a few concepts that once again belong among those to be swept away. First of all there is metaphysics. This is a matter of an Arabic deformation of the Aristotelian title 'meta ta physika', that has penetrated Western languages by way of Thomas's Commentary on the Metaphysics. The metaphysics of the thirteenth century is a philological misunderstanding. What I am doing here is not metaphysics, but something quite different. Another word which has to be cleared away, because it is used constantly without any meaning, is ontology. It comes from the seventeenth century. The word was in fact used for the first time by Goclenius in 1636. The Cartesian thinker Clauberg took care of spreading it and in the process discovered the synonym, 'ontosophy,' in order to talk about things philosophical and, incidentally, to treat God as an object, instead of as a moving factor in a meditative movement. A third term of this kind is Erkenntnistheorie or epistemology. Reinhold first speaks of a theory of knowledge in 1832. A further such word is value. It gets introduced into the language of science in dependence on Lotze by the Southwest German School (of Neo-Kantianism) at the end of the nineteenth century. I appears first in English in 1906 in a translation of the works of Brentano and attains to a certain widespread usage in the period before and after the First World War. We see, then, that the whole current modern vocabulary emerged quite late. It is a matter of the incrustation of realities, which today needs to be dissolved in order to make contact with reality again.

This first complex, therefore, which I have worked out and which should not be cut into pieces as regards either pole or the process itself enters into tension with the subject-object tension. When we construe the subject as the knowing subject, then we are following a speech usage that I believe is usual in the West: we have a consciousness of something, we speak about something, we think, we imagine something. In English it is always 'something,' and so I name this state of affairs a reality in the mode of thing-reality, which corresponds to a consciousness of something. I make the supposition that this thing-reality, which this 'something' is, this 'something' about which one is thinking, of which one speaks, and so forth, is a consequence of the fact that human consciousness is corporeally localized and that, in relation to our corporeal localization, everything of which one has consciousness, this 'something' is co-experienced as an 'outside' of this corporeal existence. The object of consciousness has to it, therefore, an aura of externality; but when one identifies this reality with the aspect of object, then there arises the problem that the subject which knows, or does not know, or talks about this object actually belongs to the same reality to which the objects belong; so that therefore the object-character, the thing-reality, is a mode of reality in relation to an attitude of consciousness which intends a truth as object. For these reasons, I name this characteristic of consciousness the 'intentionality of consciousness'. In this intentionality there is a subject of consciousness, located in a physical-concrete human being; and then objects about which he speaks, whereby one can leave open whether then are external objects of noemata in a phenomenological sense. There are always things about which one speaks.

Now we have the further problem that the subject belongs to the same reality that is supposed to be known as object—and this subject-object relationship is a further such complex. It is an event in another reality. It is neither the subject-reality nor the object-reality in its thingness, but a reality which embraces both, a comprehensive reality. For this comprehensive reality there exists philosophically, as far as I know, no commonly used expression. Nietzsche often concerned himself with it and called it the 'It'; and I will stay with this usage. In English I speak about the 'It-realty'.... In the structure of consciousness, therefore, we find two modes: a thing-reality that corresponds to the intentionality of consciousness; and an It-reality which is to be determined more closely. This 'It-reality' is an 'It' in which a thing-like consciousness occurs in the same sense in which something like the genesis of atoms and molecules, species and races and such-like occur. This means that whenever one now relates it to consciousness, this 'It-reality becomes luminous. Correlatively to intentionality, I speak, therefore about luminosity. The subject of this luminosity, in which this occurrence, 'consciousness,' happens predicatively, is not the human I, but the 'It-reality.' This becomes luminous. We are dealing with two structures in consciousness: an intentionality, of which we can say the human being is the subject; and a luminosity, of which we have to say the 'It' is the subject, and consciousness is the predicative occurrence in 'It.' When, therefore, we speak about the fact that consciousness embraces intentionality and luminosity, they should not be separated one from the other. There is then no luminosity as object of a special study about the 'It'; neither is there psychology or phenomenology as a special study about the intentionality of the subject. Human consciousness always manifests both structures.

In the context of the great history of philosophy, this has resulted in a confusion of concepts that has not been clarified until our own day. I would say the following: To the intentionality-component of consciousness there corresponds the idea which results from the concept of the concept. One formulates concepts of a reality; while the concept is thus determined by the intentionality, as regards the relation of consciousness back to its luminosity, I would like to speak of symbols. The expression 'symbol' is always determined by the dominant consciousness-component of its luminosity, of the 'It.' All that which emerges in symbols of consciousness and language is the luminosity of the 'It.'

But with both these components—intentionality and luminosity—the complex of consciousness is not complete. For what is it that we are doing here? Are we dealing with a study of intentional consciousness in which we form concepts of something? Or are we speaking in the categories of luminosity? I would say that we are doing neither the one nor the other; but we are reflecting on the complex of consciousness. We are having to do with a reflective attitude which emerges whenever one has to speak about such things. When Plato writes a dialogue, then it is partially a matter of forming concepts analytically, partially of forming a myth with symbols; and the whole offers us neither entirely an analysis nor a symbolic myth entirely. What are we dealing with in the results of reflection? I would like to speak of a further component in the structure of consciousness, which I am calling 'reflective distance.' In reflective distance the entire problem of luminosity and intentionality is now transposed into a language of reflection, in which this problem is spoken about as if there were a reality independent of reflection. Naturally, we could not talk about it if reflection were not already present as a component of consciousness, for only so can one differentiate it. But from this there arises a further problem. We can distinguish intentionality and luminosity as the structural realm in which participation in reality occurs; and then we can speak about this as if they were things about which one can make propositional statements. Thereby the risk of fragmentizing arises again. If we assume that the reflective distance and the language in which one speaks about a participation are the same language in which the experience of luminosity and intentionality along with its symbols and concepts are expressed, then we arrive at an identification of these components of reflective distance in consciousness with the participatory components which we have found here in this complex. In this case therefore we fall prey to the error of identifying the human components in the complex of participation with the reflective components directed toward the total complex. Once again, this is the mistake of the Hegelian system. The reflective I in the distance, which Plato always carefully kept separate from the participatory self, is identified with the participatory self in such a way that the intentional or the luminous element of consciousness is posited as one with the reflective element. Then you get such notions as, for example, Feuerbach's and Marx's conception (in Hegel's wake) according to which all speech about the divine is a projection of the human consciousness and full humanity only arises when this transcendent reality is taken back into human beings. I am giving you such examples here, so you can see that an immense job of enlightenment remains to be done here, in order even to be able to talk about such things.

We have come up therefore with three components in consciousness, which are always simultaneously present in various degrees of articulation and which should not be identified with one another. It is a question of a quite complicated structure of consciousness, therefore, which supposed to clarify what is to be understood here by 'complex' in such a context. The reference here to Freud is obvious, and it has also come to my attention in recent weeks. In his late works, Freud made the quite interesting observation about the 'Id,' the 'ego,' and the 'superego' that precisely the 'superego' is not set in opposition to the unconscious; but that in the 'superego' unconscious elements are also present. He calls them 'It-elements.' And this problem of an unconscious 'superego,' of a superego that operates unconsciously and that cannot be fully controlled, is also involved in a concept I have developed in another context, the 'public unconscious.' This means that any public situation is determined by the fact that, in the socially dominant forms of speech, elements that are unconscious are involved (or not) in so far as it treats of things which should be present but are not consciously articulated and so lead to disturbances manifest in every possible disorder. Heraclitus has already dealt with this matter. He distinguishes between private and public in the sense that all perspectives which have private and incomplete horizons are 'private'; whereas complete consciousness is public consciousness and should only contain elements which people factually hold in common and which can thus constitute public reality. Heraclitus calls this <u>logos</u>. Consequently, the <u>logos</u> of the philosopher, when he speaks, must find in Heraclitus the distinction between luminosity, intentionality, and reflective distance. This 'public unconscious,' I believe, is also one of the categories which has to be promulgated today. It bespeaks the fact that our society is dominated by persons who are characterized in great measure by what Heraclitus called private opinions. These private opinions create an illusionary public sphere, which engenders disorder. Against this disorder the true public sphere of meditative reality has to be achieved.

ON "THE MEDITATIVE ORIGIN OF THE
PHILOSOPHICAL KNOWLEDGE OF ORDER"

Frederick Lawrence
Boston College

As we near the end of a year of trying to read in a careful and serious fashion some of the greatest works of the West from Plato and the Hebrew Scriptures down to Nietzsche in our Perspectives program for freshmen here at Boston College, we are confronted by one of the greatest challenges of the course: to grapple with one of Nietzsche's Untimely Observations, entitled "On the Advantage and Disadvantage of History for Life." It comes like an examination of conscience for teacher and student alike. What had we been doing in the course? How had we been reading? Had we been, like those who want to create something great, putting together solid blocks of monumental meaning? Or had we perhaps approached each text in an antiquarian fashion in the attitude of those who wish to cling to the accustomed and time-honored? Or had we been so compelled by contemporary need of humankind that we could not but pursue our study of these texts in a critical way? Nietzsche's great protest invites us to reflect on what we are like as moderns overburdened with history, we who are kept from personally mustering the conditions of intelligence, reason, and responsibility needed for a truly critical study of the great works from the past. Reading him, we sense that the capacity to do critical study at this juncture would require something in the nature of a conversion, a becoming other, for which there are few examples in the contemporary academy (Voegelin, 1966b).

As you have noticed, I have used a couple of expressions, 'examination of conscience' and 'conversion,' that may be familiar to you from what is today one of the fastest growing "fields" and "fads"—the area of religious spirituality. "Spirituality" is a word coined in the eighteenth century: It was worked out to complement the overwhelming lacks in the decadent theology that had settled into the inert posture of what is now called "the manual tradition" of Roman Catholic and Protestant Orthodoxy. And, prey to the weaknesses of the theology in which it was trying to cooperate, it imported a not altogether salutary, reified understanding of a two-storied cosmos into its apprehension of the time-honored task "of despising of earthly things and the savoring only of those which are above." I am mentioning this because Voegelin is liable to call the great originative thinkers, like those studied in the Perspectives program, "Spiritualists." But when he does so, he is surely not associating himself with the provincialism "of eighteenth century rationalism and prayer"; but I believe he is bringing out that what is at stake in the critical recovery of the past is a matter of spirituality properly understood: namely, what Hans Urs von Balthasar has called "the way a person understands his or her own ethically and religiously committed existence, and the way he or she acts and reacts habitually to this understanding." Nothing primarily pious, enthusiastic, devotional or churchy about that; but rather a matter of a person's knowing and acting before God in society and in history; of how one concretely takes one's bearings in this universe; of one's living and that in the light of which one lives. In fact, Voegelin is a spiritual writer addressing the issues of spirituality today, precisely because he has undertaken the Nietzschean "examination of conscience" and is trying to articulate for us conditions of "conversion" needed for living our personal, social and historical lives in a self-transcendent fashion.

Now the title of my essay—On 'The Meditative Origin of Philosophical Knowledge of Order'—also has a 'spirituality' ring to it. You can observe that my own contribution to that title is the word, 'on,' since the rest is the title of an essay by Voegelin on which I want to focus my comments this morning.

Voegelin has been out to uncover or recover the order in history by coming to terms with the history of order and disorder. However, after doing analyses of the movements of Communism, Fascism, National Socialism, and racism, of constitutionalism, liberalism and authoritarianism, he tells us, in 1943 he had no doubt that the "center of a philosophy of politics had to be a theory of consciousness (1977:3). So far as I know, what Voegelin means by the phrase "theory of consciousness" is utterly unconventional, at least as far as the following examples are concerned: "the neo-Kantianism, the Marburg school, the value philosophy, the Southwest German school, the value-free science of Max Weber, the positivism of the Viennese school, of Wittgenstein, and of Bertrand Russell, the legal positivism of Kelsen's Pure Theory of Law, the phenomenology of Husserl." Indeed, in a striking illumination by contrast, Voegelin's account of what was missing from Husserl's phenomenology of consciousness may serve to suggest the sense of the field explored by his own theory of consciousness:

> The historical dimension (excluded by Husserl)...was not a piece of 'past history' but the permanent presence of the process of reality in which man participates with his conscious existence. Reality, it is true, can move into the position of an object-of-thought intended by a subject-of-cognition, but before this can happen there must be reality in which human beings with a consciousness occur. Moreover, by virtue of their consciousness these human beings are quite conscious of being parts of a comprehensive reality and express their awareness by the symbols of birth and death, of a cosmic whole structured by realms of being, of a world of external objects and of the presence of divine reality in the cosmos, of mortality and immor-

tality, of creation into cosmic order and of salvation from its disorder, of descent into the depth of the psyche and meditative ascent toward its beyond. Within this rich field of reality-consciousness, finally there occurs the process of wondering, questing and seeking, of being moved and drawn into the search by consciousness of ignorance, which, in order to be sensed as ignorance, requires an apprehension of something worth[y] to be known; of an appeal to which man can lovingly respond or not so lovingly deny himself; of the joy of finding and despair of having lost the direction; of the advance of truth from the compact to differentiated experiences and symbols; and of the breakthroughs of insight through visions of the prophetic, the philosophic, and the Christian-apostolic type. In brief, man's conscious existence is an event within reality, and man's consciousness is quite conscious of being constituted by the reality of which it is conscious. The intentionality is a substructure within the comprehensive consciousness of a reality that becomes luminous for its truth in the consciousness of man (10-11).

As regards the word "meditative" in our title we notice from this citation that the range of comprehensiveness of the consciousness envisaged by Voegelin's theoretic enterprise is commensurate with what he once called "the experiential complex of the meditation at the summit of which the intention of consciousness is directed not objectively through the cogitata to the contents of the world, but non-objectively to the world-transcendent ground of being" (1966a:653). The process and scope of meditation, as it was classically articulated by Augustine and Husserl, is quite explicitly crucial to Voegelin's project, because for him philosophy and theory are essentially "interpretations of experiences of transcendence." Voegelin contends that while "phenomenological philosophizing such as Husserl's is in principle oriented to the model of the experience of objects in the external world" (1981a: 464); and while "it would (not) make sense to reject the magnificent work Husserl had done in clarifying the intentionality of consciousness" (1977:10); still his own meditative project would emulate "classical philosophizing about political order" by being "equally in principle oriented to the model of noetic experience of Transcendent divine being" (1981a:464).

Voegelin has called the post-1943 enterprise "new investigations toward the philosophy of consciousness-investigations into experiences of order and its symbolic expressions, into the institutions that establish it, and finally into the order of consciousness itself" (465). In this connection Voegelin invokes a distinction between theologia mystica and theologia dogmatica documented in the Patres, in the Scholastics, and in the mystics of the fourteenth century by way of calling attention to "the difference between experiences of divine reality and the transformation of the insights engendered by the experience into doctrinal propositions" (1975:766). Thus, he understands his meditative "inquiry into the history of experience and symbolization" to be a generalized version of "the Anselmian fides quarens intellectum."

For Voegelin philosophy as <u>fides quarens intellectum</u> is cognate with philosophy as love of wisdom and has its concrete starting point in <u>philia</u>. In this sense he cites Plato's <u>Gorgias</u>: "And wise men tell us that heaven and earth and gods and men are held together by partnership (<u>koinonia</u>) and love (<u>philia</u>), by propriety (<u>kosmiotes</u>), moderation and justice; and that is the reason, my friend, why they call the whole of things by the name of <u>kosmos</u>, not of disorder (<u>akosmia</u>) or dissoluteness (<u>akolasia</u>)" (507e-508a in 1981b: 250-251). Parallel to the <u>fides caritate formata</u> of Thomas, there are Plato's experiences of transcendence and the Aristotelian <u>phronesis</u> and <u>philia</u> that Voegelin calls existential virtues (1966a:131).

The primordial matrix of meditation is participatory consciousness. It is paradigmatically actuated in experiences "of a human questioning (<u>aporein</u>) and seeking (<u>zetein</u>) in response to a mysterious drawing (<u>helkein</u>) and moving (<u>kinein</u>) from the divine side" (1981b:247). It is only within such experiences that the structure of consciousness becomes plain. The identical action of questioning and passion of being pulled involves a process of tension that transpires between poles (human and divine that may never be reified) which mutually interpenetrate one another. Together, poles and process make up what Voegelin calls consciousness as Metaxy (the In-Between), where order in society and history is experienced by concrete human beings.

A. <u>Intentionality</u>: The most obvious structural dimension of consciousness is intentionality. It is most adequately exemplified by Voegelin in sense perception of external objects in the world. Two features stand out in his analysis: (a) the <u>transitive</u> character of consciousness brought to speech grammatically in such expressions as 'consciousness of...', 'aware of...', 'thinking of...', etc.; (b) the <u>locatedness</u> of consciousness in a body in space and time, which sheds an externality upon the perceived and bestows upon the words, 'object' and 'thing' the character of 'the already-out-there-now.' "In the room the women come and go / Talking of Michelangelo." If we are or have been in the room with them, we can see, hear, smell, touch them as they walk and talk and think about an 'object' that filled a narrow strip of space and time a long time ago.

B. <u>Luminosity</u>: A second structure of consciousness, far more important for Voegelin, is called luminosity. Consciousness is an event or occurrence within a greater whole, a comprehensive reality never reducible to either the subject-pole of intentionality or its object-pole. Voegelin calls this encompassing reality 'It' or 'It-reality.' Whenever It-reality impinges on consciousness, it becomes luminous for it and endows consciousness with luminosity. The present of the thinker's consciousness is the point at which the process of reality becomes luminous for its truth: the consciousness in

On "The Meditative Origin..." / 57

its structure of luminosity is a participating in the encompassing process of the It-reality mainly by way of attunement, openness, and balanced orientation. By this dimension of consciousness we are enabled to "apprehend / The point of intersection of the timeless with the time." Nothing like the perception of women coming and going, but something more akin to "the moment in the rose garden, / The moment in the arbour where the rain beat, / The moment in the draughty church at smokefall." In other words, intentionality is only a substructure of consciousness's overall activity of participation.

C. Language: Correlative to these structures are expressions of language. The intentionality structure of consciousness tends to express itself in concepts; the luminosity structure in symbols. Concepts express or refer to objects in the external world. But symbols arise from the exegesis of the event of luminosity in participatory consciousness in which the truth of the It-reality becomes luminous. They do not refer to objects, in Voegelin's sense, but evoke movements of existence or participatory consciousness. As Voegelin has put it, then, "[t]heir meaning...is not simply a matter of semantic understanding; one should rather speak of their meaning as optimally fulfilled when the movement they evoke in the recipient consciousness is intense and articulate enough to form the existence of its human bearer and to draw him, in its turn, into the loving quest of truth" (1981b:261).

D. Reflective Distance: A further structure of consciousness must be presupposed in order for anyone to be able to thematize either the intentionality or the luminosity of consciousness and express those structures in language, namely, 'reflective distance.' This is the intrinsic reflexivity always already proper to consciousness prior to explicit acts of reflection. It is activated in meditative exegesis; or in explanations of luminosity or intentionality, etc. Just as intentionality is a substructure of participatory consciousness, so, too, reflection is secondary to participatory experience, for it is only "an orientation within the space of consciousness by which [one] can push to the limit of consciousness, but never cross those limits" (1966:58). Thus, just as the reduction of the symbolic evocation of the experience of luminosity to the thing-like clarity cognate with intentionality is the crux of "hypostatization" and of the intentionalist fallacy, so, too, the failure to distinguish between the performance of participatory consciousness in the process of reality as a whole and subsequent reconstructions of reflection leads to such terrible deformations and eclipses of reality as are found in modern theories of consciousness.

E. Perception vs. Remembering: Voegelin's thematization of the structures of consciousness, as we can see, highlights chiefly two basic kinds of cognitional operations. On the one hand, there is the sense perception of external objects, the centerpiece for Husserl's phenomenology propped on egology. And on the other, there is reflectively distanced anamnesis:

> Remembering is the activity of consciousness by which what has been forgotten, i.e., the knowledge latent within consciousness, is raised up out of unconsciousness into a specific presence of consciousness. In the Enneads (IV 3 30), Plotinus described this activity as the transition from non-articulated to articulate, self-perceiving thought. The non-articulated knowledge (noema) becomes conscious knowledge by an act of perceptive attending (antilepsis); and this antileptic knowledge is fixed again by language (logos). Remembering, then, is the process in which non-articulated (ameres) knowledge is elevated into the realm of linguistic picturability (Bildlichkeit) (to phantastikon) and through expression, in the pregnant sense of taking external shape (eis to exo), attains to linguistically articulated presence of consciousness (1966a:11).

Voegelin's overwhelming preoccupation, of course, has been with this highly complicated operation instead of simple sense perception. Not only did he not feel the need to redo what Husserl had done, but the latter operation both exhibits the different structures of consciousness in their interdependence and, more significantly, constitutes the core of meditation and so of Voegelin's method of political philosophy.

F. <u>Relatedness to the ground of being</u>: The only further structure of consciousness that I want to stress here has been expressed most beautifully in Voegelin's rendering of Aristotle's account of noetic experience:

> [M]an finds himself first in a state of ignorance (agnoia, amathia) concerning the ground (aition, arche) of his existence. Man, however, could not know that he does not know, unless he experienced and existential unrest to escape from his ignorance (pheugein ten agnoian) and to search for knowledge (episteme). Since a general term, corresponding to the later anxiety, did not yet exist in the Greek of the classic philosophers, Aristotle must characterize this unrest through the more specific terms diaporein or aporein which signify the asking of questions in the state of confusion or doubt. "A man in confusion (aporon) or wonder (thaumazon) is conscious (oietai) of being ignorant (agnoian)" (Metaphysics, 982b 18). From this restlessness in confusion arises the desire of man to know (tou eidenai oregontai) (980a 22). In the restless search (zetesis) for the ground of being (arche), then, there must be distinguished the components of desiring (oregesthai) and knowing (noein) the goal and, correspondingly, in the goal (telos) itself the aspects of object of desire (orekton) and of an object of knowledge (noeton) (1072a 30). The search, thus, is not blind; the questioning is knowing and the knowing is questioning. The desire to know what one knows to desire injects internal order into the search, for the questioning is directed toward an object of knowledge (neoton) that is recognizable as the object desired (orekton) is found (1974b:190).

Under these six headings, then, the salients of Voegelin's theory of consciousness can be found. I would now like to offer some critical reflections on that theory.

A. <u>Intentionality</u>: For me, the most questionable part of Voegelin's analysis is his treatment of intentionality along with the cognate terms, "object" and "thing." The main problem I have is with the dominance of the model of sense perception in it. I would contend that there are conscious acts which are intentional, but which simply may not be helpfully compared to sensory acts. Thus, just as Voegelin criticized the narrowness of Husserl's choice of examples of auditory perception in relation to the matter of consciousness as a stream and the constitution of time-consciousness, so I would question the adequacy in his analysis of the intentionality structure of using sense perception to provide the main specification of the meaning of intentionality. Why not use wonder or questioning as the key to the meaning of intentionality? This would be more in harmony with the centrality of the participatory experience of the tension towards the ground of being as well as with the dynamics of remembering. Surely it can be shown that the range of conscious and intentional activities at work in concrete human questing involves irreducibly distinct yet complementary kinds of questions and coordinate acts which arise in response to these questions. These acts are also intentional, but what they intend most radically is not "the already-out-there-now," but being. Acknowledging the fuller range of wonder's dynamic structure bursts open the meaning of intentionality as restricted to the experience of discrete acts of sense perception of the already-out-there-now. For if intentionality springs from primordial wonder, the potential range of consciousness as intentional matches that of the questioning response to the mysterious pull of transcendent mystery.

1. <u>Correlative revision in notion of consciousness</u>: Shifting from sense perception to wonder as the key to human consciousness even as intentional allows us to understand consciousness itself in a manner that only confirms Voegelin's basic insight into consciousness as "the In-Between reality of the participatory pure experience" (1977a:171). To begin with, it lets us expand Voegelin's brief against "the immanentizing language of a human consciousness which, as a subject, is opposed to an object of experience" to the specific reality of human knowing. When Voegelin's analysis of conscious intentionality is radicalized by asking about what we as concrete persons actually do when we ask and answer questions, we find that human knowing is not a simple, mysterious confrontational relationship between subject and object on the analogy of sensing, but a structured activity composed of distinct elements none of which alone constitutes knowledge by itself, since each element is merely a constitutive part of the whole we name knowledge. At the same time we discover that consciousness as a strictly inner experience of oneself and one's cognitive and appetitive acts is nothing like an inward look, but a property common to those acts, in spite of the differences in

their contents, which is evidently not shared by other bodily acts like the growth of our hair and fingernails. We grasp, too, that it is on the basis of this similarity that the acts of sensing, inquiring, understanding, critical reflection, and judgment are not disconnected, but get integrated into unified acts of knowing. Wonder, inquiry, direct insight, etc., form a natural unity because they are conscious. And so consciousness, which is activated by and in accord with these manifold and diverse processes, achieves their immanent identify, even as it itself goes beyond each of them by providing them their constant point of reference. The inner experience of consciousness secures our presence to what we intend by conscious acts; but through these acts of apprehension and appetite, it is also operative as a concomitant and irreducible presence to self.

2. <u>Conscious Intentionality and Self-transcendence</u>: The present analysis of conscious intentionality agrees with Plato, Aristotle, and Voegelin that the central manifestation of consciousness <u>as human</u> is the specific tension of spirit we call wonder. This disturbance, this unrest within us that renders Hume's world of sensations puzzling and questionable is rooted in human consciousness as that by which we are originally given to and experience ourselves, prior to any intelligent and reasonable response, and prior even to any determination and formulation of wonder by an inner word. For doesn't wonder mean that we are given to ourselves as an infinite potentiality that strives toward the whole of being in a dynamic movement? And isn't consciousness basically just this presence of ourselves to ourselves in unrestricted and active potentiality, the self-presence, that is to say, of a principle of infinite questioning and questing whose measure and standard is determined by the goal of infinite understanding and love that is the divine mystery? If these questions can be answered affirmatively, then consciousness is an unrestricted dynamism that underpins and penetrates all our knowing. "It is an unrestricted intention that intends the transcendent, and a process of self-transcendence that reaches it" (Lonergan, 1967a:231). This is what makes possible that "ceaseless action of expanding, ordering, articulating, and correcting itself" that Voegelin tells us activates "conscious existence" as an "event in the reality of which as a part it partakes" (1977a: 221).

3. <u>The Meaning of "OBJECT", "THING", "REALITY"</u>: If we turn, then, to a basic meaning of the words, "object," and "thing", it becomes clear that they should not be made equivalent to the correlative of sense perception. Indeed, to think of "thing-ness" as spatio-temporal bodiliness and of objectivity as "the already-out-there-now" is to fall into a conception of reality and of being that is irrational. This is not to dispute the spontaneous evidence of an external world or the rationality of propositions based

upon such evidence, but to suggest that problems of immanentism and relativism are only resolved within the unrestricted horizon of the question. With that horizon, then, reality is the object of those acts by which the unrestricted desire to know is actuated and by which the quest for knowledge becomes actual knowledge. A more exacting examination of our mental processes of coming to know shows how sense perceptions provoke a structure of several intellectual operations that are "related to sensitive operations, not by similarity, but by functional complementarity" (Lonergan 1967a:234): inquiry, understanding, conceiving, critical reflection, reflective insight, and judgment. Once we acknowledge this structure of consciousness as under the sway of wonder, it becomes difficult to limit the meaning of "object", "things", and "reality" to the "already-out-there-now" grasped by sense perception. Instead they are what we apprehend by insight and reasonable affirmation.

This conception of "object", "thing", "reality" as the objective of the dynamic structure of our pure desire to know does not entail any bondage to a principle of immanence:

> Because the intention [of consciousness] is unrestricted, it is not restricted to the immanent content of knowing, to Bewusstseinsinhalte; at least, we can ask whether there is anything beyond that, and the mere fact that the question can be asked reveals that the intention, which the question manifests, is not limited by any principle of immanence. But answers are to questions, so that if questions are transcendent, so also must the meaning of corresponding answers (Lonergan, 1967a:230).

B. Luminosity: I would like to return now to the subject of the luminosity-structure of consciousness. On Voegelin's account, luminosity tends to function as a counterfoil to the limitations ascribed by him to the intentionality structure on the model of sense-perception. This procedure casts suggestive light on aspects of consciousness that cannot be accounted for from the vantage of the perceptualist model's presupposition of the subject/ object split as ultimate. On the one hand it goes beyond the voluntarist connotations of attentiveness: we notice the women as they come and go, we hear them speaking of Michelangelo, whereas luminosity has more the character of supervening on or occurring to us, like the moment in the rose-garden. On the other hand, whereas the intentionality of sense perception tends to get absorbed with what we are focally aware of, however much luminosity may determine our focal or explicit consciousness at any time, it is always principally operative as implicit or tacit background awareness, to which we respond by articulation in word and deed. Consequently, events of luminosity can never be exhausted by acts of focal awareness, or be brought fully into the foreground of consciousness. We can only become more attuned to luminosity.

I am basically in agreement with these insights into luminosity as profiled against the intentionality-structure of sense perception. But I would prefer not to dissociate luminosity from intentionality, but rather to specify it too in terms of wonder and questioning. With Lonergan I would rather say: "questioning not only is about being but is itself being, being in its Gelichtetheit (luminousness), being in its openness to being, being that is realizing itself through inquiry to knowing that, through knowing, it may come to loving" (1967b:206). What differentiates human being from other conscious beings is that it is a notion of its goal. This means that in wonder or in the pure desire to know, consciousness experiences itself precisely as spiritual or intellectual, inasmuch as the unrestrictedness of its intention--completely universal and utterly concrete--entails an anticipatory grasp of the intelligibility, the unconditionality, and the absoluteness of being. Since, with Aristotle and Aquinas, we are speaking here of an infinite potency (potens omnia facere et fieri), this immediately given luminosity of wonder is not the luminosity of that which it is already, but rather of what in its empty totality it anticipatorily apprehends and longs for, and what it dynamically seeks. I would say that what is most basically meant by luminosity, therefore, is wonder as involving an experiential knowledge of itself (ex parte subjecti) that has not been objectified and so does not involve the objective content of any cognitive act; instead it is an implicit awareness of itself as the principle of such acts, and so it is an inexhaustible background, a tacitly performative awareness. When it is unfolded in particular questions for intelligence, reasonableness, and deliberation, it does so as involuntary occurrence, supervening on sense awareness; and its fulfilment in direct and reflective acts of understanding manifests these same traits: we cannot will either questions or insights; we can only be more or less open to them.

It follows that I would agree in principle with what Voegelin was getting at when he contended that concrete human consciousness "is not an apriori structure, nor does it just happen, nor is its horizon a given,... [but] a ceaseless action of expanding, ordering, articulating, and correcting itself" (1977:4). The reason for this is that luminosity as wonder is a factual constituent of human consciousness, but in Lonergan's words, "it does not consistently and completely dominate human consciousness. It is a fact to which man has to advert, which he has to acknowledge and accept, whose implications for all his thinking and acting have to be worked out and successfully applied to actual thinking and actual acting" (1967c:199-200). In short one has to make one's actual horizon match the factual yet merely potential range of primordial wonder's unrestrictedness.

Furthermore, by equating luminosity with primordial wonder as questioning, we can preserve Voegelin's insight into the role of the divine pole in luminosity's achievement by stating simply that God is the ultimate ground of knowledge, but that human beings know because luminosity is an immanent source of transcendence. We know because of our own intelligence whose immanent structures possess a transcendent dynamism. In Thomas Aquinas's formulation, human intelligence is a "created participation of uncreated light." This strengthens Voegelin's idea that attending to luminosity subverts the intentionalist-hypostatizing assumption of the ultimacy of the subject/object split. From the perspective of luminosity as an immanent source of transcendence, the so-called problem of knowledge is transformed. It is not a matter of the subject "in here" moving to objects "out there", but of our moving from an "infinite potentiality commensurate with the universe towards a rational apprehension that siezes the difference of subject and object in essentially the same way that it seizes any other real distinction" (1967:88).

Once we have grasped the distinction between God as the ground of knowledge and human luminosity as an immanent source of transcendence, the possibility also opens up of drawing a radical distinction between classes of horizon-enlargement that may actually arise when the orientation and performances of finite human consciousness really do coincide with the demand implicit in the pure desire to know and "an ultimate enlargement [that] alone approximates to the possibility of openness defined by the pure desire" (Lonergan, 1967c:200). This distinction is intimately connected with Plato's breakthrough to the Beyond as the creative, divine ground and Aristotle's description of the ground of being as "eternal, immovable, and separate from the change of sense perception" (Voegelin, 1974:245). Thomas Aquinas discerned this distinction from the difference between the adequate object of our desire, namely, videre Deum per essentiam (to know God by his essence), and the proportionate object of our knowledge, namely, realities intrinsically conditioned by space and time (Lonergan, 1967d; 1956:634-730).

On account of the limitations of the proportionate object of our knowing (experienced in the endlessness of the questions for intelligence, reasonableness and responsibility that can be raised), our natural knowledge of God will only admit of analogical—or, to use Voegelin's term, symbolic—fulfilment. But we still naturally desire and are open to essential knowledge of God who is not intrinsically conditioned by space and time. In Thomas's framework, this means the fulfilment of our natural desire to know is supernatural. Accordingly, the class of actual enlargements of horizon "implicit in the very structure of human consciousness," is really distinct from its "ultimate enlargement, beyond the resources of every finite consciousness, where there enters into clear view God as unknown, when the subject knows God face to face" (200). For Christians, the existence of such a fulfilment is known by faith in the beatific vision. But the theoretical distinction between nature and supernature helps the believer to articulate the gift and elevating character of grace, while guarding against any suspicion that God's self-communication is alien or extrinsic to the horizon of human being (Lonergan, 1974).

As one engaged in <u>fides quarens intellectum</u>, Voegelin's stress has been upon the conditions for concretely closing the gap between luminosity as a principle of achievement and luminosity as achievement in human living: especially, conversion and the existential virtues of faith, hope, and love present in the mature and good person (<u>spoudaios aner</u>, <u>daimonios aner</u>). He has made abundantly clear that symbolic expression of these conditions in noetic or pneumatic exegesis never reduces them solely to human accomplishments. Luminosity as achievement, concretely and as a matter of fact, is inseparable from grace; whereas the use of the distinction between nature and supernature would often seem to have been motivated by doctrinaire polemics. Moreover, Voegelin's emphasis has been upon the psychic, the imaginal, and the linguistic aspect of luminosity's effectiveness, especially from the side of the divine pole. On the one hand, "Reality is an act of divine mythopoesis that becomes luminous for its truth when it evokes the responsive myth from man's experience" (Voegelin, n.d.:17; cp. 1974a:13). On the other hand, "[One's] responsive pursuit of [one's] questioning unrest to the divine source...however, if it is to be responsive indeed to the divine mover, requires the effort of articulating the experience through the appropriate language symbol" (1974:244). For Voegelin, then, luminosity becomes effective in and through a revelatory trail of compact and differentiated symbols, and especially in breakthrough symbolisms "of the prophetic, the philosophic, and the Christian-apostolic type" (1977:11).

I find the overwhelming power of this approach to lie in the following features:

(1) it leaves no doubt that the radical alternatives in human living are indeed the two loves Augustine called <u>amor sui</u> and <u>amor Dei</u>;

(2) it also resists any attempt at separating the divine and human components in the universe that <u>de facto</u> exist;

(3) it avoids any denominational or sectarian narrowing of the universality of God's loving concern for every human individual;

(4) it locates humanity within the framework of a free creation and a free salvation by a mystery of love and awe;

(5) it is sensitive to the way God enters into creative communication with humanity through disposing the pre- and un-conscious depths of the human psyche;

(6) it makes mystagogy the core of philosophy.

My own difficulty with this enterprise arises chiefly from the fact that for Voegelin the radical exegetical alternatives are symbolic or conceptual; but the conceptual tends to get consigned to 'intentionalism.' This tends to mean that any exegesis or instrumental act of meaning which tries both to rigorously distinguish between meaning and meant and to settle the probable or certain status of what is meant by any given experiences or expressions gets neglected. Of course, I do not mean to deny that as a matter of fact, many or even most instances of such theoretical and critical intent have derailed into intentionalist hypostatizing. I also agree that reification of divine mystery is reprehensible. It is also true that the constitutive and communicative functions of meaning and the symbolic apprehension of meaning cognate with these functions by which we make ourselves and the human set-up are of far greater moment to human existence than the cognitive function of meaning by which we distinguish between verbal, notional, and real distinctions (Lonergan, 1972:76-81). But the latter, too, can both be motivated by a deliberate and conscientious pursuit of understanding and truth and give rise to a systematic interpretation of truths previously apprehended and interpreted only symbolically (81-84, 95-99, 335-353). For example, Thomas's theory of habitual and actual, operative and cooperative grace was such a systematic interpretation. Thomas neither aimed at nor achieved system in the rationalist sense of a set of self-evident and necessary truths from which necessary conclusions follow; or of some precisely defined and permanent system of eternal verities. This theoretic articulation of the mysteries of faith did not seek to master, but to open a window for the heart and mind into the mysteries by understanding and conceiving an "intermediate, imperfect, and analogous intelligibility" (339).

Aquinas's distinction between the lumen naturale as an obediential potency and the light of faith, of prophecy, and of glory as absolutely supernatural elevation, only made it possible for Christian thinkers to integrate the threefold personal self-communication of divinity with an evolutionary vertical finality as it enters human consciousness in a theoretical view that distinguishes natural and supernatural components in a way that is no less reasonable than distinguishing the sub-atomic particles studied by physics from the molecules and compounds investigated by chemistry (Lonergan, 1974:16). But besides letting Christian thinkers understand the graciousness of a loving God more differentiatedly, it also "issued an invitation to reason to grow in consciousness of its native power, to claim its proper field of inquiry, to work out its departments of investigation, to determine its own methods, to operate on the basis of its own principles and precepts" (1956:527). Again, it meant that the theoretical, critical, and methodical exigencies of human conscious intentionality in history could be differentiated from the transcendent exigence in order to serve it more adequately in hearing and responding to the Cosmic Word of God (Lonergan, 1972:82-83). It meant that the dynamics of human self-appropriation and self-realization could be thematized more adequately so that the specific meaning of the moral and intellectual conversions implicit in religious conversion can be more satisfactorily explicated (241-243). All of these possible and actual outcomes are chiefly instances of differentiation in experience and symbolization. They get derailed if they lead to separations; but they are for the sake of integration. And their point of integration is the unity of consciousness both as differentiated and as intellectually, morally and religiously converted.

WORKS CONSULTED

Lonergan, Bernard
- 1956 — Insight. A Study of Human Understanding. New York: Philosophical Library.

- 1967 — Verbum: Word and Idea in Aquinas. Ed. by D. Burrell. Notre Dame, IN: University of Notre Dame Press.

- 1967a — "Cognitional Structure." In Collection: Papers by Bernard Lonergan. Ed. by F.E. Crowe. New York: Herder and Herder, 221-239.

- 1967b — "Metaphysics as Horizon." In Collection, 202-220.

- 1967c — "Openness and Religious Experience." In Collection, 192-201.

- 1967d — "The Natural Desire to See God." In Collection, 84-85.

- 1972 — Method in Theology. New York: Herder and Herder.

- 1974 — "Natural Knowledge of God." In A Second Collection. Ed. by W. Ryan and B. Tyrrell. London: Darton, Longman and Todd, 117-133.

- 1974/6 — "Mission and the Spirit." In P. Huizing and W. Bassett, eds., Experience of the Spirit. Concilium 9:69-78.

Voegelin, Eric
- 1966a — Anamnesis. Zur Theorie der Geschichte und Politik. Muenchen: R. Piper.

- 1966b — "Die deutsche Universitaet und die Ordnung der deutschen Gesellschaft." Wort und Wahrheit 8/9:497-518.

- 1974 — "Reason: The Classic Experience." The Southern Review 10:237-264.

- 1974a — The Ecumenic Age. Volume 4 of Order and History. Baton Rouge: Louisiana State University Press.

- 1975 — "Response to Professor Altizer's 'A New History and a New But Ancient God'." Journal of the American Academy of Religion 43:765-772.

- 1977 — "Remembrance of Things Past." In his Anamnesis. Trans. and ed. by G. Niemeyer. Notre Dame, IN: University of Notre Dame Press, 3-13.

- 1981a — "In Memoriam Alfred Schütz." In P.J. Opitz and G. Sebba, eds., The Philosophy of Order. Essays on History, Consciousness and Politics. Stuttgart: Klett-Cotta, 463-465.

- 1981b — "Wisdom and the Magic of the Extreme: A Meditation." The Southern Review 17:235-287.

- n.d. — "The Beginning of the Beginning." Unpublished.

THEOLOGY'S SITUATION:
QUESTIONS TO ERIC VOEGELIN

Robert M. Doran
Marquette University

I do not consider myself an expert in the thought of Eric Voegelin. But I have found myself deeply enriched, instructed, and challenged by many of his writings, especially the four presently available volumes of Order and History. In the present paper, however, I hope not so much to specify the precise influence of Voegelin on my own work as to outline the development of that work to date and to employ that outline as a point of departure for dialogue with Voegelin and his students. The positive influence that Voegelin's work has had on my own will be apparent in the outline.

My work to date is a series of preliminary investigations anticipating a contemporary systematic theology. These prior investigations have not yet come to an end, but the general contours are already apparent. The work is an exercise in the theological functional specialty, foundations (Lonergan, 1972: chap. 11). It offers a heuristic structure for understanding three distinct but interrelated dialectical processes constitutive of the situation which a systematic theology addresses, where that situation is in general a matter of the dialectic of authenticity and inauthenticity. These processes are the dialectic of the subject, the dialectic of community, and the dialectic of culture. Each process is a dialectic because it is an unfolding of linked but opposed principles of change (Lonergan, 1957:217). But the overall dialectic of authenticity is a dialectic of contradictories. It is resolved only by a choice between alternatives. The dialectics of the subject, of community, and of culture are dialectics of contraries. Both poles must be affirmed, each in its proper place. In a dialectic of contraries, the condition of the possibility of an integral dialectic lies in a third principle that stands above the two principles internally constitutive of the dialectic. The distortion of the dialectic of contraries through the ascendancy of one of its two internally constitutive principles is rooted in the maldevelopment or breakdown of this third, synthetic principle, and results in inauthenticity, as contradictory to the authenticity constituted by the integral dialectic of contraries.

Thus the dialectic of the subject is internally constituted by the two principles of neural demand functions and dramatically patterned intelligence (Lonergan, 1957:189-196), and the condition of its integrity is an adequate and in the last analysis universal antecedent willingness (Lonergan, 1957: 598, 610-611, 623-624). The dialectic of community is internally constituted by spontaneous intersubjectivity and practical intelligence (Lonergan, 1957: 214-218), and the condition of its integrity is culture (Lonergan, 1957: 236-238). And the dialectic of culture itself is internally constituted by cosmological and anthropological basic assumptions of meaning and value informing given ways of life, and the condition of its integrity is a differentiated soteriological vector that moves from above downwards in human consciousness (Voegelin, 1956:56; Lonergan, 1975). Each dialectic of contraries is an instance of the tension of limitation and transcendence constitutive of all genuine development in the universe (Lonergan, 1957: 472-475). Neural demand functions, spontaneous intersubjectivity, and cosmological insights are the principles of limitation in the respective dialectics of the subject, community, and culture; and dramatically patterned intelligence, practical intelligence, and the anthropological principle are the respective principles of transcendence. Willingness, culture, and the soteriological differentiation of consciousness are higher syntheses conditioning the possibility of integrity in the respective dialectics of contraries. The dialectic of contradictories has ultimately to do with the integrity or disintegration of these higher syntheses.

The situation to be addressed by any systematic theology mediating not in oratione obliqua from the past into the present but in oratione recta from the present into the future is constituted by the actually functioning relations among these dialectics. The dialectic of culture, moreover, operates on two levels: a spontaneous level of everyday transactions, which this dialectic shares with the dialectics of the subject and of society, and a reflexive level of scholarly and scientific objectification, which reflects, among other things, on all three everyday dialectics. From a normative point of view, the everyday functioning of the three dialectics in their relations with one another constitutes the infrastructure of the situation, and the reflexive objectifications the superstructure. When this relationship of infrastructure and superstructure is upset, the situation is distorted. For then something that belongs in the infrastructure usurps the prerogatives of the superstructural level of culture.

Theology is superstructural. Through the use of special theological categories, it mediates the meanings and values constitutive of Christian witness, fellowship, and service with the (sometimes dialectically reoriented) general categories that theology shares with other superstructural disciplines (Lonergan, 1972:281-293). The mediation is a matter not of correlation, as is erroneously presupposed by many contemporary theological methodologies (see Lawrence, 1981), but of creative systematic construction. It is conducted in an atmosphere of interdisciplinary collaboration. It is governed by foundational reflection on converted interiority. And it heads toward a basic science of humanity, of which theology is but a part, and which is concerned not only with the understanding but also with the making of history (Lonergan, 1957:227, 233-234). The foundations of the mediation lie in interiorly differentiated consciousness, which is the source of the derivation and purification especially of the general categories but also, when extended to include religious and Christian self-appropriation, of the special categories (Lonergan, 1972:292-293).

The first phase of my work was concerned with the dialectic of the subject. I have recently completed the intitial stage of a study of dialectic of community, and am only beginning to work out the dynamics of the dialectic of culture. It is with this third dialectic that the work of Eric Voegelin may prove to be most provocative of insight. But his writings have helped me to understand better what I was doing in my work on the dialectic of the subject, and have posed the central problem with which I had to deal in my reflections on the dialectic of community.

THE DIALECTIC OF THE SUBJECT

My work on the dialectic of the subject, I realized after reading Voegelin, is geared to providing among other things the basis for what he calls a psychology of orientations as opposed to a psychology of passional motivations. A psychology of orientations is "a science of the healthy psyche, in the Platonic sense, in which the order of the soul is created by transcendental orientation." A psychology of passional motivation is a "science of the disoriented psyche which must be ordered by a balance of motivations." It is incomplete, "in so far as it deals only with a certain pneumopathological type of man" (Voegelin, 1952:186). More precisely, I have attempted to articulate the reorienting influence of the intentionality analysis of Bernard Lonergan on the science of the sensitive psyche, and then to argue that this reoriented science—reoriented from a psychology of motivations to a psychology of orientations—complements the intentionality analysis from which it is derived, by providing a further dimension of interiorly differentiated consciousness. Such an articulation implies, I believe, a differentiation of the Greek psyche, employed interchangeably by Voegelin as "soul" or "psyche," into transcendentally oriented intentionality and the sensitive psyche.

The basis for the reorientation of the science of the psyche I found in the recognition by Lonergan in his post-1965 writings of the existence and indeed primacy of a fourth level of intentional consciousness that is distinct from the three levels uncovered in the cognitional analysis of Insight. Existential consciousness governs the authenticity of the empirical, intellectual, and rational levels of consciousness, and sublates them into its own concern for world- and self-constitutive praxis. The fourth level of consciousness is a notion of value. It intends the human good, which is a concrete process, at once individual and social, and which consists in the making of human history, the flowering of human authenticity, the fulfilment of human affectivity, and the direction of human labor to a good of order and to particular goods that are really and not just apparently worth while (Lonergan, 1972: 52). These potential values are apprehended in intentional feelings (Lonergan, 1972:30-34), which themselves function in a relationship of reciprocal evocation with symbols: "A symbol is an image of a real or imaginary object that evokes a feeling or is evoked by a feeling" (Lonergan, 1972:64). Existential self-appropriation, the understanding, knowledge, and self-conscious orientation of the subject as a deliberating, evaluating, deciding subject can, I concluded, be greatly aided by employing these relations among symbols, feelings, and values, and so by using one's spontaneously produced symbolic manifestations as a clue to insight into the intentional feelings that themselves are revelatory of one's spontaneous preferential scale of values (Doran, 1977:17-113).

The scale of values is determined in accord with a criterion of self-transcendence.

> Not only do feelings respond to values. They do so in accord with some scale of preference. So we may distinguish vital, social, cultural, personal, and religious values in an ascending order. Vital values, such as health and strength, grace and vigor, normally are preferred to avoiding the work, privations, pains involved in acquiring, maintaining, restoring them. Social values, such as the good of order which conditions the vital values of the whole community, have to be preferred to the vital values of individual members of the community. Cultural values do not exist without the underpinning of vital and social values, but none the less they rank higher. Not on bread alone doth man live. Over and above mere living and operating, men have to find a meaning and value in their living and operating. It is the function of culture to discover, express, validate, criticize, correct, develop, improve such meaning and value. Personal value is the person in his self-transcendence, as loving and being loved, as originator of values in himself and in his milieu, as an inspiration and invitation to others to do likewise. Religious values, finally, are at the heart of the meaning and value of man's living and man's world (Lonergan, 1972:31-32).

A psychic conversion that establishes a working commerce between the neural demand functions and dramatically patterned intentional consciousness can enable a subject intent on existential self-knowledge to ascertain, and to participate in guiding and orienting, the development of his or her spontaneous scale of value-preferences (Doran, 1972, 1981).

The commerce of neural demand functions and intentional consciousness is dialectical, where a dialectic is conceived as "a concrete unfolding of linked but opposed principles of change" (Lonergan, 1957:217). Dramatically patterned imagination and intelligence operate preconsciously in the selection of images for insight, and of their concomitant affects. They function as a censorship over neural demands for psychic representations. The censorship can be either constructive or repressive. It is constructive if it

> selects and arranges materials that emerge in consciousness in a perspective that gives rise to an insight; this positive activity has by implication a negative aspect, for other materials are left behind and other perspectives are not brought to light; still, this negative aspect of positive activity does not introduce any arrangement or perspective into the unconscious demand functions of neural patterns and processes (Lonergan, 1957:192).

The censorship is repressive if

> its positive activity is to prevent the emergence into consciousness of perspectives that would give rise to unwanted insights; it introduces, so to speak, the exclusion of arrangements into the field of the unconscious; it dictates the manner in which neural demand functions are not to be met; and the negative aspect of its positive activity is the admission to consciousness of any materials in any other arrangement or perspective (Lonergan, 1957:192).

The dialectic is described as follows:

> The contents and affects emerging into consciousness provide the requisite aggregate of events of a determinate kind; these events originate from two principles, namely, neural demand functions and the exercise of the constructive or repressive censorship; the two principles are linked as patterned and patterning; they are opposed inasmuch as the censorship not only constructs but also represses and, again, inasmuch as a misguided censorship results in neglected neural demands forcing their way into consciousness; finally, change is cumulative, for the orientation of the censorship at any time and the neural demands to be met both depend on the past history of the stream of consciousness (Lonergan, 1957:217).

Voegelin has called our attention to the need of developing a vocabulary for understanding, not psychopathology, but pneumopathology: "spiritual disease has never been made the object of systematic inquiry and no suitable vocabulary has been developed for its description" (1975:263). In this regard, the instructive point about the heuristic structure that Lonergan offers for understanding and appropriating psychic processes lies in the dialectical relationship of neural demand functions and dramatically oriented <u>intentionality</u> at the ground of the events that constitute the experience of the sensitive psyche. The key issue is what one <u>wants</u>. There is an aberration of understanding resultant upon the love of darkness. The issue is one of <u>willingness</u>, which is more radically a spiritual orientation than it is a psychic state of affairs.

> [E]ffective freedom itself has to be won. The key point is to reach a willingness to persuade oneself and to submit to the persuasion of others. For then one can be persuaded to a universal wilingness; so one becomes antecedently willing to learn all there is to be learnt about willing and learning and about the enlargement of one's freedom

from external constraints and psychoneural interferences. But to reach the universal willingness that matches the unrestrcted desire to know is indeed a high achievement, for it consists not in the mere recognition of an ideal norm but in the adoption of an attitude towards the universe of being, not in the adoption of an affective attitude that would desire but not perform but in the adoption of an effective attitude in which performance matches aspiration (Lonergan, 1957:623-624).

Within such a perspective, psychotherapy should be conceived regulatively as the enlargement of one's effective freedom from the psychoneural interferences that block one's performance as a self-transcending attentive, intelligent, rational, and morally responsible person. Real therapy of the psyche, then, is an extension of an ever greater antecedent willingness into the domain of the neural demand functions themselves. The movement of conversion to willingness is a movement from above downwards in consciousness (Lonergan, 1975), and so is radically a therapy of pneumopathology before it becomes one of psychopathology. Moreover, the science of the sensitive psyche must be grounded in an explanatory objectification of the exigencies of the notions of intelligibility, truth, being, and value that constitute the perennial and transcultural structure of the human spirit. In this regard at least, then, my attempts to date to reorient the science of depth psychology on the basis of Lonergan's intentionality analysis are also attempts to meet Voegelin's call for "a science of the healthy psyche, ... in which the order of the soul is created by transcendental orientation."

That transcendental orientation, of course, is for Voegelin ultimately the orientation to the divine ground. My own reliance on Lonergan is in accord with this insistence. "There is to human inquiry an unrestricted demand for intelligibility. There is to human judgment a demand for the unconditioned. There is to human deliberation a criterion that criticizes every finite good. So it is ... that man can reach basic fulfilment, peace, joy, only by moving beyond the realms of common sense, theory, and interiority and into the realm in which God is known and loved" (Lonergan, 1972:83-84). The sensitive psyche participates in the dynamism of transcendentally oriented intentionality.

In my efforts to articulate the function of the psyche as what Voegelin would call a sensorium of transcendence (1952:75), I have engaged in a fundamental critique of Jungian archetypal psychology, arguing principally that Jung's notion of archetypal symbols suffers from the same limitations that Voegelin finds characteristic of the cosmological symbolization to which the archetypes in fact correspond. "Not much is really clear beyond the experience of participation and the quaternarian structure of the field of being, and such partial clearness tends to generate confusion rather than order, as is bound to happen when variegated materials are classified under too few heads" (Voegelin, 1956:3). In fact, Jungian immanentism clouds even the experience of participation in being, incurs the danger of the inflated self-assertion that, I fear, is the ultimate meaning of Jung's work, and reduces the cosmological quaternarian field (gods and man, world and society) to a matter of the self-enclosed psychological functions of thinking, feeling, sensation, and intuition. Jung is correct in disengaging a dimension of transpersonal symbolization which he calls archetypal, a dimension unaccounted for in Freudian psychoanalysis. But transpersonal symbolization is itself twofold. Archetypal symbols—a term to which I assign a less inclusive connotation than does Jung—are taken from nature and imitate nature, thus manifesting the participation of psyche and organism in cosmic rhythms and processes, and providing access to the retrieval through interiorly differentiated consciousness of the partial truth of the cosmological societies. Anagogic symbols, however, even when taken from nature as in some eschatological symbolizations, manifest either the anthropological principle that our transcendental orientation to the divine is the measure of the order of the soul, and the order of the soul the measure of society (Voegelin, 1952:66-70), or the soteriological truth of existence in Christ Jesus, existence redeemed from the distorted dialectic of the subject and invited then to participate in the redemptive law of the cross. (The latter truth, I believe, is not sufficiently differentiated by Voegelin from the anthropological principle that reached its first clear articulation in Greek philosophy. We will see more of this later, when we discuss the dialectic of culture. For the moment, it is sufficient to indicate that the antecendent willingness that is the condition of the possibility of an integral dialectic of the subject is a fruit of this soteriological vector in human consciousness, whether this soteriological vector be expressly acknowledged as such or not.)

There is one further aspect of Voegelin's thought that will prove helpful to me in any future work that I do on the dialectic of the subject. It emerges most clearly in his as yet unpublished chapter, "The Beginning of the Beginning," and has to do with the dialectic—for Voegelin, paradox—of consciousness as at once intentionality and luminosity (Voegelin, 1983). It is this dialectic (of contraries) that in a way lies at the origin of my attempts to complement Lonergan's work with an articulation of psychic conversion. These attempts began with a question regarding the relations between the later Heidegger and the early Lonergan. I have not yet reflected enough on Voegelin's thoughts regarding this dialectic of consciousness to say more than that I suspect that psychic conversion and Lonergan's intellectual conversion represent the means of retrieving, respectively, and in interiorly differentiated consciousness, Voegelin's consciousness as luminosity and his consciousness as intentionality. Voegelin's insistence on consciousness as luminosity represents, I believe, a valuable complement to Lonergan's analysis of intentionality; but students of Voegelin who desire greater precision on consciousness as intentionality should turn to Lonergan, whose objectification of this dimension of consciousness is unparalleled in accuracy, clarity, and explanatory power, and, incidentally, bears remarkable resemblances to Voegelin's retrieval of the classic experience of reason (Voegelin, 1974).

THE DIALECTIC OF COMMUNITY

"Society" is a generic term embracing five interrelated elements: spontaneous intersubjectivity, technological institutions, an economic structure, the polity, and culture. Culture has two levels: the everyday and the reflexive. The source of technological institutions, the economic structure, and the polity lies in practical intelligence. The actually functioning relations among these elements determine the health or pathology of a society. As my work on the dialectic of the subject was concerned with the constitution of the healthy psyche, so my reflections on the dialectic of society have an equally normative purpose, and so are geared toward a regulative and heuristic understanding of the constitution of a healthy society. The work on the dialectic of the subject was a matter of implementing Lonergan's transcendental method so that it grounds a reoriented science of psychic sensitivity; that on the dialectic of community implements the same method to ground a reoriented science or set of sciences of society.

The dialectic of community, as we learn from Lonergan, is internally constituted by the two linked but opposed principles of human intersubjectivity and the commonsense practicality that is responsible for technological institutions, the economic structure, and the legal and political arrangements of a society. The dialectic is integral when the changes resulting from these two principles take account of and keep pace with one another. It is distorted to the extent that either principle gains the ascendancy in the determination of these changes. The condition of an integral dialectic of community lies in neither principle itself but in culture: infrastructurally, in the meanings and values that inform everyday transactions, and superstructurally, in the reflexive objectifications of these meanings and values in the various human sciences, in philosophy, and in theology. The integrity of culture, in turn, is grounded in the "dimension of consciousness" that Lonergan calls cosmopolis: a dimension that is "neither class nor state, that stands above all their claims, that cuts them down to size, that is founded on the native detachment and disinterestedness of every intelligence, that commands man's first allegiance, that implements itself primarily through that allegiance, that is too universal to be bribed, too impalpable to be forced, too effective to be ignored" (Lonergan, 1957:238). From such a "dimension of consciousness, a heightened grasp of historical origins, a discovery of historical responsibilities," there can emerge "an art and a literature, a theatre and a broadcasting, a journalism and a history, a school and a university, a personal depth and a public opinion, that through appreciation and criticism give men of common sense the opportunity and help they need and desire to correct the general bias of their common sense" (Lonergan, 1957: 241). For that general bias is the radical source especially of the distortions of the integral dialectic of community that prevail in the current situation.

General bias distorts the dialectic of intersubjectivity and practicality in the direction of practicality. It is more radically disintegrative of society than is the group bias that displaces the dialectic in the direction of intersubjectivity, for it generates a longer cycle of decline. The cycle promoted by group bias generates its own reversal more quickly, for the practical ideas excluded or mutilated by powerful groups are championed later by the disadvantaged, whose sentiments "can be crystallized into militant force by the crusading of a reformer or a revolutionary" (Lonergan, 1957:225), while the reversal of the cycle generated primarily by general bias depends on implementing "ideas to which all groups are rendered indifferent" (Lonergan, 1957:226) by the pretentions of practical shortsightedness to the imperious omnicompetence of instrumentalized rationality. Such ideas include those "that suppose a long view or that set up higher integrations or that involve the solution of intricate and disputed issues" (Lonergan, 1957:228), and so that demand the subordination of common sense to a higher specialization of human intelligence. That higher specialization, which is at once theological, philosophic, and human-scientific, is grounded in "the discovery, the logical expansion and the recognition of the principle that intelligence contains its own immanent norms and that these norms are equipped with sanctions which man does not have to invent or impose" (Lonergan, 1957:234). This principle is implemented on the superstructural level of culture by developing an empirical, critical, and normative human science, where "empirical" includes preeminently taking account of the data of consciousness, and on the everyday level in the cultural values that would sustain and support the integral dialectic of intelligence and intersubjectivity. Cosmopolis has a responsibility for the integrity of culture on both levels. It fails to meet this responsibility on the superstructural level to the extent that it sanctions the subordination of human science to the biased intelligence of those that produced the presently available data. It fails on the everyday level if it does not resist the deterioration of culture into "a factor within the technological, economic, political process, ... a tool that serve[s] palpably useful ends"; and to the extent that it does not promote culture as "an interdependent factor that passes a detached yet effective judgment upon capital formation and technology, upon economy and polity" (Lonergan, 1957:237).

The relations among the constitutive elements of society can be further understood, I have found, if we reflect in more detail on the scale of values mentioned in the previous section. The levels of value are related to each other in a number of ways. Among these sets of relations I would posit two that are particularly germane to the present discussion: a relation of differentiation and creativity that obtains from below upwards, and a relation of conditioning and enablement that obtains from above downwards. From below, problems in the recurrent realization of values at a lower level can frequently be solved only by the creation of new arrangements at a higher level. Thus a breakdown of the equitable distribution of vital values to the whole community can at times by solved only by the creation at the level of social values of new technological realities, or by the adjustment of the economic system, or by a change at the level of law or politics. Moreover, it may be the case that the changes demanded at this level of social values are so extensive as to demand the differentiation and implementation of transformed cultural values, at either the everyday or the reflexive level of culture, or at both. These changes may themselves be so demanding as to require a conversion to greater personal integrity on the part of persons who would be originating values. And personal integrity cannot be sustained without the effective operation of and cooperation with divine grace, and so without a deepening and more pervasive religious conversion.

These relations of creativity and differentiation from below upwards obviously imply a set of relations of conditioning and enablement from above downwards. Religious values condition the possibility of personal integrity. Personal integrity conditions the possibility of a culture that neither retreats into an ivory tower nor capitulates to imperious practicality. Such a culture conditions the possibility of the integral dialectic of community in the establishment of the good of order. And this dialectic conditions the possibility of the effective and recurrent distribution of vital values to the whole community. Within the dialectic of community itself, moreover, the elements emergent from commonsense practicality—technology, the economy, and the polity—are related in a similar fashion. The problem of a recurrent realization of particular goods evokes technology or capital formation, technology evokes the economy, and the economy evokes the polity (Lonergan, 1957:208-209); but technology is for the sake of meeting recurrent vital desires, the economy is for the sake of the effective functioning of the technological system, and politics is for the sake of the integral dialectic between economic and technological arrangements, on the one hand, and intersubjective spontaneity on the other hand.

The position just enunciated differs on several counts from the Marxist one. First, Marx located the basic dialectic of society as a dialectic ultimately of contradictions within practicality—namely, between technology (the forces of production) and the economy (the relations of production), whereas Lonergan has articulated it as a dialectic of contraries between practicality and intersubjectivity. Second, this difference implies a subordination of practicality to the dramatic constitution of the human world as a work of art. Third, this subordination implies the possibility of genuine and autonomous integrity at the level of culture, and the responsibility of culture for the integrity of the dialectic of community. Fourth, the legal and political domains constitute an element of the infrastructure, not of the superstructure of society. The superstructure is constituted by the reflexive level of culture. When the normative scale of values is respected, culture is not an ideological domain created for the conscious but mendacious representation of the underlying conflict between forces and relations of production, but is a pursuit of the meanings and values that, among other things, will develop the human capacities by which the integral dialectic of community can be preserved or restored. The genuine function of politics is not to guarantee by ideologization the capitulation of practical intelligence to group ethos or of speculative intelligence to instrumental practicality, but, on the contrary, to persuade individuals and groups to subordinate and adapt their vital spontaneities to genuinely practical ideas and to persuade the proponents of these ideas to respect the legitimate demands of individual and group spontaneity. Finally, and most radically, my position differs from the Marxist one in the role it assigns to the possibility and significance of personal integrity sustained and deepened by God's grace.

The relations that I have posited among the levels of value may be employed, I believe, as a means of understanding and discussing some of the problems that arise in contemporary political philosophy. These problems, in turn, force a further clarification of the integrity of the scale of values itself. In both of these areas, moreover, questions for dialogue with Eric Voegelin arise.

Liberal democratic and Marxist political philosophies share in common one structural feature that is illuminated by the scale of values: in them there is found either a negligence of or a scepticism regarding the autonomy of religious, personal, and cultural values, and so a tendency to collapse the effectively operative scale into the two more basic levels of social and vital values. When this neglect affects the actual workings of a liberal or Marxist society, legal and political institutions slip out of the infrastructure and become the lowest rung, as it were, of a mendacious superstructural edifice erected for the sake of preserving a distorted dialectic of community in which intersubjectivity is neglected in its autonomous capacity as a formative principle of society and is twisted through group bias into becoming an ally of a practicality distorted by general bias. Legal and political dimensions of society are then determined by economic relations rather than devised to effect the unfolding of an integral dialectic between these relations and intersubjective groups. Politics should be the infrastructural institution whereby the whole community can be persuaded by rational argument and symbolic example to exist and change in the tension of the opposites of vital spontaneity and practical ideation and decision. Under the dominance of a group bias conscripted by general bias, however, it becomes rather an instrument of the distortion of the dialectic through a displacement of that tension. Slipping out of the infrastructure, it becomes a mendacious determinant of the meanings and values that inform the way of life of segments of the community. Thus it usurps the prerogatives of culture. The public determinants of meaning and value that would arise from the pursuit of the beautiful, the intelligible, the true, and the good are evacuated from the cultural scene. They retreat into the margins of society. The effective culture becomes merely an instrument of distorted practicality. The superstructure becomes a surd when the political specialization, defaulting on its legitimate and necessary infrastructural function, invades the domain of culture. Genuine culture surrenders its function of autonomously determining the meanings and values that, through political integrity, would otherwise govern the economy and the institutions of technology as dialectical counterparts of spontaneous intersubjectivity. The meanings and values that govern the way of life of the society become nothing more than the projections of a distorted societal dialectic. As culture retreats, morality and religion follow suit. The good, which is the objective that guides and orders the pursuit of the true, the intelligible, and the beautiful, is rendered inefficacious in the structuring of the cultural and social order. Religious values are either explicitly denied and even forbidden in the public domain, as in some Marxist states, or twisted into perverse supports for the distorted culture and society, as in American civil religion. The entire structure is upset by the derailment of the political, a derailment rooted in the loss of the tension between practicality and intersubjectivity which it is the responsibility of culture to inform and of politics to implement. Only the integrity of a culture that refuses to become proximately practical and expedient, yet that insists on remaining on the scene, can prevent such distortions from taking place.

If this is the upshot of liberal and Marxist political philosophies, classically inspired political philosophies, while they stress the integrity of culture and at times, as with Voegelin, of the personal and religious levels of values as well, exhibit a problem contrary to that of the liberal and Marxist positions: namely, a truncation or relative neglect of the two more basic levels of value. Their acknowledgment of questions of distributive justice and the economic order is by and large negative: they criticize with great acumen the pretensions of liberal and Marxist ideologies to promote the just social order to which they claim to be devoted; but they neglect the extent to which their own oversight of the constitutive function of vital and social values in the entire hierarchy of values can render the classical tradition susceptible to an unwitting conscription by default or retreat into especially the liberal distortions of the dialectic of community. More precisely, while classically inspired political philosophies correctly affirm that the social order is a derivative of operative cultural values and that the latter are conditioned by personal integrity or the lack thereof, and thus while they display a sensitivity to the relations that obtain from above downwards among the levels of value, they do not recognize that the relations from below upwards may call for more than a reaffirmation of the cultural values of the classical tradition. Perhaps these values, however necessary they may be, must today be sublated into an entirely new horizon that institutes a quite novel set of cultural values commensurate with the dimension of the social problem.

The crucial link in the scale of values vis-à-vis the difficulties contained in both liberal and Marxist political philosophies, on the one hand, and in classically inspired political philosophies, on the other hand, has to do with the relations of reflexively objectified culture, i.e., of the superstructure, to the entire infrastructure of everyday cultural values, politics, the economy, technology, and spontaneous intersubjectivity. The opposed tendencies manifest that the relations of religious, personal, and cultural values among themselves and the relations between social and vital values are easier to grasp and affirm than are either the relations of the three higher levels to the two more basic levels or the relations within culture itself between the superstructure and the everyday. A political philosophy must be created which, while maintaining the permanent validity of the classical tradition, sublates this tradition into a higher synthesis characterized as well by a concern for the questions, though not the solutions, of liberalism and Marxism.

The distortions instituted by liberalism and Marxism provide the very conditions for developing such a philosophy. For, precisely as a result of the skewed dialectic of community sponsored by the competing and escalating imperialisms of late capitalism and state socialism, these distortions are now global, and in a systemic fashion. The relations from below upwards among the levels of value begin with a global network of if-then relationships at the levels of technological institutions, economic systems, and political relations. The need for a globally accepted social order can be met only if crossculturally generated cultural values are established to insure the integrity of the social dialectic on a global scale. These values must be elaborated by cosmopolitan collaboration at the superstructural level, but they must be effective as well at the everyday level of culture. The means for elaborating them lie in the appropriation, philosophic reference-specification, and integration of the various regionally inherited cultural values that constitute the human heritage. Such an enormous task of cosmopolitan collaboration, however, will depend for its integrity on the appropriation through interiorly differentiated consciousness of the transcultural psychic and intentional constituents of authentic human participation in the search for direction in the movement of life. And this transformation at the level of personal value will itself depend upon both the clarification and the enrichment of authentic religiosity that is demanded if the entire task is to succeed. Central to this development will be dialogue and cooperation among the major religions of the world.

The link between superstructure and infrastructure, and that between cultural values in general and the social order, are reestablished in such a perspective. The global nature of the contemporary exigence for social order calls for the development of a new set of cultural values as the condition of the possibility of a just social order, where justice is a function of the integral dialectic of spontaneous intersubjectivity and practical intelligence. When the social order becomes global, cultural values must become world-cultural, if minds and hearts are to be equal to the tasks set by the conditions of global technological, economic, and political interdependence. A problem at a lower level of value is not to be met simply by mere restructuring at that level nor even by a retrieval of traditional cultural values unmediated by attention to the concrete infrastructural realities that set the context of the problem in the first place.

It is important at this point to distinguish our anticipations of a world-cultural humanity from the various tendencies that for Voegelin constitute the modern gnosticisms. Whether they be intellectual or political in nature, the gnosticisms immanentize the teleological and axiological components of Christian hope (Voegelin, 1968:99-100). Immanentizing the teleological constitutes progressivism, immanentizing the axiological constitutes secular utopianism, and immanentizing both constitutes the activist mysticism deriving from Comte and Marx. As we will see in more detail in the next section, our anticipation of a world-cultural network of communities not only does not immanentize Christian eschatology, but takes its stand on the world-transcendent objective of Christian hope. Moreover, while the gnosticisms tend to reflect a less differentiated spirituality than that which can be discovered in the classical and Christian sources of Western civilization, our anticipation of an ecumenic consciousness entails the advancing differentiation brought about by intellectual and psychic self-appropriation. Finally, while the gnosticisms are meant to become mass movements, our anticipation recognizes the difference between the fuller realization of ecumenic consciousness in cosmopolitan explanatory self-appropriation and the everyday post-interiority transformations brought about by successful communication on the part of the cosmopolitan minority, and sharply distinguishes its own vision of a global network of communities living in accord with the integral scale of values from the mass movements catalyzed by the libido dominandi.

Nonetheless, one critical comment regarding Voegelin's understanding of the modern gnosticisms is in order. He says:

> No matter to which of the three variants of immanentization the movements belong, the attempt to create a new world is common to all. This endeavor can be meaningfully undertaken only if the constitution of being can in fact be altered by man. The world, however, remains as it is given to us, and it is not within man's power to change its structure (1968:100).

While we have reason for dissatisfaction with the world in which we live, nonetheless, says Voegelin, besides attributing our dissatisfaction to the intrinsic drawbacks of the situation, "it is likewise possible to assume that the order of being as it is given to us men (wherever its origin is to be sought) is good and that it is we human beings who are inadequate" (1968:86-87).

Surely a distinction is in order here, one that would advance the positions and reverse the counterpositions in the modern gnosticisms (Lonergan, 1957:388). From the ontology implicit in many of the modern gnosticisms can be drawn the insight that is constitutive of modern historical consciousness in general: the human world, mediated and constituted by meaning and motivated by value, is the product of human insights, judgments, and decisions. Human praxis *is* constitutive of being: not originatively creative of its elemental structure, but responsibly constitutive of the character of the human world as good or evil. The real human world as it is and the good human world as it ought to be are not coincident. In the world mediated by meaning, the notions of being and of value are not coincident. Surely the movement from the real human world as it is to the good human world as it ought to be is grounded in a transformation of ourselves; but self-constitution is coincident with world-constitution. A philosophy of world-constitutive praxis need not violate the order of the soul masterfully disengaged in Voegelin's retrieval of classical sources. The conversion positions on praxis characteristic of classically inspired political philosophies and the world-transformation positions present but counterpositionally formulated in the modern gnosticisms can be integrated with one another by forcing the meaning of the integral scale of values as a guide to authentic praxis itself. The implications of this will be most evident in the exigence that emerges for the development of crossculturally generated values to inform a global social order constituted by the integral dialectic of community.

THE DIALECTIC OF CULTURE

In this section I am merely stating in very rudimentary and hypothetical fashion a quite recent insight that emerged from several years of considering what Voegelin has written about cosmological, anthropological, and (to a far less extensive degree) soteriological symbolizations of the experience of order. The insight is this: as there is a dialectic of the subject between neural demands and dramatically patterned intentional consciousness, a dialectic whose principle of integrity lies in a universal antecedent willingness, and as there is a dialectic of community between intersubjectivity and practicality with its synthetic principle in culture, so there is a dialectic of culture itself between cosmological and anthropoligical insights, with its synthetic principle of integrity lying in the soteriological vector which comes to maximal clarity in Christian revelation and which it is the function of theology at any given time and place to mediate with the prevailing cultural matrix so as to promote the integrity of the dialectic of culture. Moreover, this soteriological vector is the source of the universal willingness and of the integral culture that are the principles of integrity, respectively, for the dialectics of the subject and of community.

In <u>Israel and Revelation</u> Voegelin enunciates a set of three principles that he uses to understand and relate the experiences of symbolizations of order that appear in the course of human history. These three principles are:
  (1) The nature of man is constant.
  (2) The range of human experience is always present in the fullness of its dimensions.
  (3) The structure of the range varies from compactness to differentiation (1956:60).

Following Voegelin let us call the range of experience that is always fully present but never fully differentiated the search for direction in the movement of life; "life is experienced as man's participation in a movement with a direction to be found or missed" (1971:63). And let us risk the judgment that the participatory quality of the experience constitutes consciousness as luminosity, and the search for direction consciounsess as intentionality.

Not only is life experienced as a movement with a direction that can be found or missed. In addition, everything depends on finding the direction and following it, each step of the way. This nuclear element of all experience is at the base of culture. Cultural order and the self-understanding informing it are a function of the search and of the incremental answers to it arrived at in the course of history. No matter how compact or differentiated an individual's consciousness or a culture's self-understanding may be, the ordering symbols that express the meaning of a way of life are always a function of this "original experience" of consciousness.

The structure of the range of this experience, Voegelin says, varies from compactness to differentiation. Compact cosmological symbolizations find the paradigm of order in the cosmic rhythms. This order is analogously realized first in the society, and social order provides the framework determining individual rectitude. Cultures minimally or maximally informed by a differentiation of insight and rational reflection from the sensitive flow, on the other hand, have expressed the experience of life in either incipient or highly developed philosophies. Then the aspired-to world-transcendent measure of integrity is the standard for the integrity of the individual, and the well-attuned individual measures the integrity of the society. Such is the basic structure of anthropological truth.

There is a basic and ineradicable tension between cosmological and anthropological truth. It is another instance of the dialectical tension of limitation and transcendence. An anticipatory and purely descriptive understanding of this tension may be arrived at by distinguishing the different experiences of time that permeate the two ways of experiencing and understanding the participatory engagement in the movement of life. It would seem that cosmological truth is rooted in the affective and so biologically based sympathy of the human organism with the rhythms and processes of nonhuman nature, whereas anthropological differentiations are implicitly or thematically constitutive of history as a process involving the contribution of human insight, reflection, and deliberation. From a purely descriptive point of view, the difference appears to be one between cyclical and linear time. If we start from the present ecological crisis generated by the technologies of societies whose scientific expertise is ultimately dependent on the theoretic differentiation of a Western variant of the anthropological breakthrough--however sharply modern science differs from classicist ideals (Lonergan, 1967)-- we see that, while Western cultures have pursued scientific and technological expertise to such an extent as to lose affective sympathy with the rhythms and processes of nature, less technologically advanced cultures, while maintaining this affective sympathy, have succumbed too massively to the rhythms and processes with which they feel themselves to be in harmony. The ecological crisis is due, it seems, to our allowing the apparent linearity of humanly constituted history to play fast and loose with the apparent cycles of nature, and to interfere with them in a cavalier fashion that introduces a fourth, mechanomorphic process of experience and symbolization. Cultures, on the other hand, that have not undergone the axial transformation of theoretic differentiation, have allowed the rhythms of their own cultural lives to be determined too exclusively by the affective sympathy they enjoy with the cycles of nature, so that their experience, if not interfered with by alien expansionism, is nonlinear and to that extent ahistorical. Because the only linearity they experience is due to alien intrusion, their sense of historical self-constitution is more negative than positive: it is radically a sense of the destruction of their own culture, an experience of their victimization by cultures affected by a contrary distortion of the dialectic of community.

In actual fact, nonhuman nature is not strictly speaking cyclical, nor is history precisely linear. If nonhuman nature were cyclical, it would display no emergence of novelty. And if history were strictly linear we could not account for the conditioning of later events by the potentialities inherent in earlier events. The whole concrete universe is informed by an intelligibility that Lonergan calls emergent probability. In nonhuman nature as well as in human history there are neither cycles nor linear sequences of ever new events, but schemes of recurrence that have a certain probability of emergence and a quite distinct probability of survival (Lonergan, 1957:chap. 4). Nonetheless, the emergence and survival of schemes of recurrence in nonhuman nature differ from the emergence and survival of schemes of recurrence that can be changed by the execution of free decisions based on new insights. What we are dealing with here is a difference not between cyclical and linear time but between different probabilities of emergence and survival due to the presence or absence of human intelligence, rationality, and decision.

When a culture is in affective sympathy with the relatively fixed schemes of recurrence in nonhuman nature, it displays a profound respect and even reverence for the exigencies of those schemes and regards them as exhibiting something like a sacred order. Care will then be taken not to violate these exigencies, a care that has to be described as religious. But the same culture is liable to be burdened with a fatalistic conception of its own historical life. It will regard human society as subordinate to the same schemes of recurrence or, it appears, cycles, that inform the process of the cosmos. The capacity of insight and decision to change society and history by introducing new shemes of recurrence into a distinctly human and so intelligent emergent probability, is liable to be overlooked. Such an oversight, of course, today makes such a culture an easy prey for domination by those of a different persuasion, who do acknowledge and employ practical insight and decision in their capacity to change the course of history. Particularly is this the case if the historically-minded group is insensitive to the affective sympathies of the cosmological culture with the rhythms and processes of nature. Cultures and peoples with an affective ecological sympathy with nature thus tend to a mythical or magical view of human affairs, seeing themselves as massively subordinate to and reliant on cosmic powers for the determination of their destinies. Their distrust in or ignorance of the power of insight and freedom to change the course of human events is exploited by expansionist imperialist ambitions of whatever variety. In fact, the clash of mentalities and cultures is a conflict between a way of life too closely identified with nonhuman schemes of recurrence, on the one hand, and an inflated self-constitutive process too sharply divorced from these schemes of recurrence, on the other hand. In the cosmological societies we find a displacing of the tension of limitation and transcendence in the direction of limitation, and in the technologically advanced societies a displacement of the same tension in the direction of transcendence. Contrary distortions of the integral dialectic of community confront one another under these circumstances.

The acknowledgment of the power of understanding and freedom to change both history and nature is a constitutive feature of the rise and success of modern science. Yet that very process is itself dependent on a theoretic differentiation of consciousness that long antedates the modern scientific revolution, however different classical ideals of science may be from modern objectives. In this sense it may legitimately be asked if the distortion of the integral dialectic of society in the direction of transcendence that is characteristic of technologically advanced societies is not rooted in an inherent danger immanent in the anthropological breakthrough itself. The cosmological tendency to identify too closely and in the last analysis fatalistically with the rhythms and processes of nonhuman nature is, I believe, readily intelligible due to the human organism's radical participation in precisely those schemes of recurrence and the human sensitive psyche's radical participation in the human organism. What is not so clear is why the mechanomorphic distortion of the same dialectic in the direction of transcendence is rooted in an exclusivism of anthropological truth to at least the same extent that the cosmological distortion is grounded in the fatalistic temptation inherent in cosmological truth. If we consider this question we will be able to understand why the integrity of the dialectic of culture can be grounded neither in cosmological truth alone nor in anthropological truth alone, but in some third process of experience, insight, symbolization, conceptualization, reflection, judgment, deliberation, and decision that we will call soteriological, and that grounds the integrity of the dialectic of cosmological and anthropological truth.

What we must try to understand is why anthropological truth without cosmological truth is apt to become <u>eventually</u> mechanomorphic distortion, and so to promote a relatively posthistoric mode of existence counterbalancing the relatively prehistoric existence of the cosmological societies. Historical existence is normatively constituted by an integral dialectic of limitation and transcendence. But the prehistoric distortion of that dialectic is more readily intelligible than the posthistoric. What is it about anthropological truth itself that renders it susceptible to mechanomorphic derailment, and so to a reversal of the axial advances achieved in the anthropological breakthrough? What is the internal flaw constitutive of this breakthrough that, unless guarded against by a set of defensive circles, lessens its probability of survival? Why is this diminishing probability of survival not to be understood as a reversion to cosmological cycles, as Voegelin seems to suppose (1956:126-133), but as a fall into posthistorical mechanomorphism? Finally, why is it the case that <u>only</u>

"a society in existence under God is in historical form" (Voegelin, 1956:132), and what does this realization say about the crucial significance of the soteriological vector with respect not only to the cosmological form of existence—this Voegelin begins to explicate quite profoundly in Israel and Revelation—but also to the anthropological?

The key to the potential derailment of the anthropological breakthrough is to be found, I believe, in the fate of the myth and the subsequent loss of the experience not so much of consciousness as intentionality but of consciousness as luminosity, not so much of the search for direction but of the movement in which life participates and in which intentional consciousness searches for, finds, and misses direction. Voegelin has displayed the sensitivity of Plato to the fate of the myth, and so the fate of the sensitive symbolizing psyche and its energic compositions and distributions, under the impact of the anthropological breakthrough to the order of the soul as the measure of society and to the world-transcendent ground as the measure of the order of the soul. But that sensitivity is precarious, and with its loss or neglect there arises the forgetfulness of the divine measure exhibited even by the sophistic antagonists of Plato's Socrates. The myth is the permanent transcendental guarantee of consciousness as luminosity, as the experience of participation in the movement of life, as a demand for attunement with what is lasting in being. And consciousness as luminosity is the permanent transcendental guarantee of the obligation of consciousness as intentionality to find the direction in the movement of life. The loss of the myth is the loss of the consciousness of the "It-reality" (Voegelin, 1983) within which intentionality is authentically oriented by the intention of intelligibility, truth, and goodness to the "Thing-reality" partially constituted by world-constitutive praxis. The loss of the myth is the source of the derailment of intentional consciousness by general bias into the immanentization of the modern gnosticisms.

In Psychic Conversion and Theological Foundations I tried to show that the neglect of the sensitive psyche, which I am here arguing to be the source of the participatory luminosity displayed in the myth, is as radically responsible for the longer cycle of decline as is the derailment of intelligence into the shortsighted omnicompetence displayed by Lonergan as the general bias of common-sense practicality; and I explained the foundational role of a transcendental aesthetic in the constitution of the self-appropriation of what I now, following Voegelin, would call consciousness as luminosity. In fact the anthropological breakthrough resulted, in Plato, in a transformation of the myth; in parallel fashion, the generalized empirical method that results from the self-appropriation of consciousness as intentionality is required for an accurate self-appropriation of consciousness as luminosity: psychic analysis depends for its integrity on intentionality analysis. But, as I have argued from the beginning of my project, intentionality analysis must be complemented by psychic analysis. The self-appropriation of rational self-consciousness makes possible, but also requires, "a new Christian philosophy ... of mythical symbols ... that would make intelligible ... the myth as an objective language for the expression of a transcendental irruption, more adequate and exact as an instrument of expression than any rational system of symbols" (Voegelin, 1975:22). The anthropological breakthrough to the differentiation of insight and reason from the sensitive flow and of explanation from description is so powerful that it could result in a more or less grave neglect of the constitutive contribution of the sensitive flow itself, a neglect in the understanding of existence that will lead to the loss of consciousness as luminosity and to the truncation of consciousness as intentionality into the instrumental manipulation of Thing-reality within a horizon no longer constituted by the experience of participation in It-reality. Voegelin's Plato, of course, did not succumb to this danger. But was he tempted to it (Voegelin, 1957:133)? For there is inherent in the axial differentiation a tendency to forget its partiality, and to reject rather than sublate and transform that from which the new clarifications are differentiated. Contra Voegelin, then, may we not root the modern gnosticisms more profoundly in a potential derailment in the anthropological breakthrough than in a supposed ambiguity in the Christian symbols and promise of salvation? In fact, I wonder whether Voegelin does not himself imply as much when we writes:

> Philosophy and Christianity have endowed man with the stature that enables him, with historical effectiveness, to play the role of rational contemplator and pragmatic master of a nature which has lost its demonic terrors. With equal historical effectiveness, however, limits were placed on human grandeur; for Christianity [emphasis added] has concentrated demonism into the permanent danger of a fall from the spirit--that is man's only by the grace of God--into the autonomy of his own self, from the amor Dei into the amor sui. The insight that man in his mere humanity, without fides caritate formata, is demonic nothingness has been brought by Christianity to the ultimate border of clarity which by tradition is called revelation (1952: 78-79).

The substantiating of this position will demand a more explanatory presentation of the differentiation of the soteriological from the anthropological either than appears in Voegelin's work or than I am prepared to offer at present. The incipient soteriology of Voegelin is with respect to deliverance from cosmological-imperial existence. A similar study of the soteriological in relation to the anthropological reaching for the divine ground remains to be done. And when it is done, it must show the influence of the soteriological on the integrity of the cosmological-anthropological tension that constitutes the dialectic of culture. Such a study would begin, I believe, not with culture itself, but with the person as originating value. There it would show the soteriological as the condition of the possibility of the integral dialectic of the subject between neural demand functions and dramatically patterned intentional consciousness, and so between the two radical sources, respectively, of cosmological and anthroplogical truth. And because the integrity of culture itself is the condition of the possibility of the integral dialectic of community, the soteriological dimension of participation in the movement of life is the radical source of the integrity of all three of the dialectics that we have discussed in this paper, grounding the integral dialectic first of the subject (personal value), then of culture (cultural value), and finally of community (social value). This would make of Christian foundational and systematic theology a more comprehensive and exact form of reflection on this participation than is the philosophy that articulates the eros for the divine ground. And yet the Christian theologian can perhaps find no better source in the contemporary scene for an understanding of, and a challenge to, a life of authentic reflection on the experience of participation in a movement that has direction that can either be found or missed, than is offered in the rich meditations that have been shared with us by Eric Voegelin.

WORKS CONSULTED

Doran, Robert M.
- 1977 *Subject and Psyche: Ricoeur, Jung, and the Search for Foundations*. Washington, D.C.: University Press of America.

- 1981 *Psychic Conversion and Theological Foundations: Toward a Reorientation of the Human Sciences*. Chico, CA: Scholars Press.

Lawrence, Frederick
- 1981 "Method and Theology as Hermeneutical." In *Creativity and Method: Essays in Honor of Bernard Lonergan*. Ed. Matthew Lamb. Milwaukee: Marquette University Press, 79-104.

Lonergan, Bernard
- 1957 *Insight: A Study of Human Understanding*. London: Darton, Longman, and Todd.

- 1967 "Dimensions of Meaning." In *Collection: Papers by Bernard Lonergan*. Ed. Frederick E. Crowe. New York: Herder and Herder, 252-267.

- 1972 *Method in Theology*. New York: Herder and Herder.

- 1975 "Healing and Creating in History." In *Bernard Lonergan: Three Lectures*. Ed. R. Eric O'Connor. Montreal: Thomas More Institute, 55-68.

Voegelin, Eric
- 1952 *The New Science of Politics*. Chicago: University of Chicago Press.

- 1956 *Order and History*. Volume 1: *Israel and Revelation*. Baton Rouge: Louisiana State University Press.

- 1957 *Order and History*. Volume 3: *Plato and Aristotle*. Baton Rouge: Louisiana State University Press.

- 1968 *Science, Politics, and Gnosticism*. South Bend, IN: Gateway.

- 1971 "The Gospel and Culture." In *Jesus and Man's Hope*. Ed. D. C. Miller and D. y. Hadidian. Pittsburgh: Pittsburgh Theological Seminary, 59-101.

- 1974 "Reason: The Classic Experience." *The Southern Review* 10:237-264.

- 1975 *From Enlightenment to Revolution*. Ed. John H. Hallowell. Durham, NC: Duke University Press.

- 1983 "The Beginning of the Beginning." Unpublished.

THE SIGNIFICANCE OF VOEGELIN'S WORK FOR
THE PHILOSOPHY OF SCIENCE

Patrick H. Byrne
Boston College

I would like to remark this evening upon directions which Prof. Voegelin's reflections upon the order of history have opened up for the philosopher of science. Probably the most significant event in recent philosophy of science has been the publication of Thomas Kuhn's The Structure of Scientific Revolutions. There has been much debate about the soundness of Kuhn's positions, which I do not wish to enter into at this time. However, the significance of the book, I believe, comes down to this: philosophy of science from now on must be reflection on the history of science. Kuhn's own attempt to reflect in this way and the ensuing debates have revealed, furthermore, that most current modes of philosophizing are poorly adapted to this new task. This problem arises from the fact that most current modes of philosphizing stand within the tradition of Kant and Lessing characterized by the slogan that "One does not gain knowledge of necessity through reflection on contingency (e.g., history)."

By taking a different point of departure, Prof. Voegelin has provided us with an important standard for philosophical reflection on history. In particular, his way of identifying 'hypostatization' as the detatchment of symbols from originating experience of participation both explains the current dilemma in philosophy of science and shows a way beyond it.

It explains the current dilemma, for modern philosophers of science have tended to reflect on results of particular investigations, and to interpret method as what leads to that kind of result. This has led, among other things, to the embarrassing "proofs" of the absoluteness and necessity of Euclidean geometry, Newtonian time, determinism, and so on. Prof. Voegelin's model would lead the philosopher of science to study the developing methods of modern science, not as restricted to results, but as modes of participation in the community of Being. To provide a more concrete idea of what I mean, let me reflect for a moment upon the path which leads from Galileo to our present.

In his Two New Sciences, Galileo explains that he is concerned to begin a new science. What he regarded as new in his science was the use of mathematics to reach scientific knowledge of phenomena in mechanics (i.e., tensile properties of solid materials) and local motion, a great many of which had not been noticed let alone demonstrated. Galileo justified his introduction of mathematical modes of thought into these fields of science by stating, "it is evident that for this as for any other eternal and necessary property, purely mathematical demonstrations can be produced that are no less rigorous than any others." By this statement Galileo reveals his allegiance to, not his abandonment of, the Aristotelian tradition on science—the quest for eternal, necessary truths. Yet in order to transfer that tradition into mathematics, Galileo has to oppose the 'common notion' that deviations of concrete phenomena from mathematical expectations are due to imperfections of 'matter.' His dialogue reveals, instead, that such deviations are due to faulty mathematical reasoning giving rise to those expectations. Anticipating this revelation, he boldly writes, "Here I do not know whether I can declare, without risking arrogance, that even recourse to the imperfections of matter, capable of contaminating the purest of mathematical demonstrations, still does not suffice to excuse the misbehavior of machines in the concrete as compared with their abstract ideal counterparts. Nevertheless I do say just that, and I affirm that abstracting all imperfections of matter and assuming it to be quite perfect and inalterable and free from all accidental change [will nevertheless show that behaviors of machines and materials will not be independent of scale]."

Clearly, a more careful exegesis of this moment in history is required than can be given this evening. Yet a few remarks are possible:

(1) The new sciences oppose the common opinion about 'matter.' The symbol, 'matter' along with the symbol 'abstraction' has a history which must be sought to understand Galileo's statement.

(2) Galileo resists the arrogance of the 'common' which blinds itself to the wondrous intelligible patterns immanent in phenomena through its complacency that it already knows their 'nature.'

(3) But Galileo also attempts to abolish the normativity still present in the distorted symbol of 'matter', and attempts to transfer all knowledge of the 'eternal and necessary' to the mathematician. In brief, the 'imperfections' of matter are assumed to be humanly perfectible (i.e., completely subsumable under the range of humanly conceivable relations), rather than signs of the mystery of the Beginning and the Beyond immanent in nature.

(4) This attempt leads Galileo into the ancient problems associated with the manner in which mathematical 'objects' relate to sensible 'objects,' particularly in regard to motions of projectiles and pendula. As a result, Galileo tries to save his project by recourse to the position that modern new sciences must abstract from imperfections "in order to make use of them in practice." In so

doing, Galileo vitiates his own attempt to free science for the authentic search for order, and opens it to the deformations of a search for imposition of human limited interest upon the 'It,' to the deformations of modern gnosticism.

While Galileo's science was new, his mathematics was not; it is the mathematics of Eudoxus, Euclid and Apollonius. Yet in his own time were the stirrings of a new mathematics, called 'analysis' by its originators. This new mathematics found its place within the Galilean project, and one finds similar tensions between the quest for method open to true order and the reduction of true order to current results in the development of analysis. On the one hand, the path from Vieta through Descartes, Newton, Liebniz, Euler, Fourier, Cauchy and Cantor exhibits a progressive movement away from the fixation on what Prof. Voegelin has called 'thing reality' toward ever more subtle forms of ordering functions, as well as increasing awareness that 'limit' is an intrinsic dimension of these forms of ordering. The introduction of statistical and relativistic methods has made limitation before the Beyond an intrinsic part of the human scientific quest. Finally, the modern sciences opened onto the mystery of the Beginning: the impossibility of asking about the time and place of the beginning of the universe. On the other had, one simultaneously finds the arrogance of Vieta, Descartes and Laplace for whom every question is susceptible of answer in terms of 'a simple analytical expression,' and the pragmatism and even sophistry of Newton and Leibniz in arguing the truth of their methods.

This approach to reflecting on the history of science suggests the need, however, for a further differentiation within what Prof. Voegelin has called "the paradox of intentionality and luminosity." The consciousness of the modern scientist is indeed participation in the community of being, a "something in a comprehending reality," but it is not principally a matter of intending a reality over against its embodiment. This is the normative element in Galileo's resistance to the 'common.' Rather, the scientist's consciousness is a participation in the 'It,' which is oriented toward intention of non-embodied yet finite intelligible relations.

This all, of course, is extremely sketchy and only suggests a line of investigation. Yet it is Prof. Voegelin's work which has opened up this as a possible direction for the philosophy of science.

RESPONSES AT THE PANEL DISCUSSION
OF "THE BEGINNING OF THE BEGINNING"

Eric Voegelin
Stanford University

[The following is a transcription of Prof. Voegelin's responses to questions raised at the panel discussion that was part of the March 1983 conference at Boston College. Both the questions posed by members of the panel and those that came from other participants in the conference have been condensed.]

In response to a question about his use of the term, symbol:

The term 'symbol' is of course a term which has acquired a lot of meanings in the course of history. The question now is, can it be used for the purposes for which I am using it, without getting into real misunderstandings? I try to give symbol the meaning of expressing the consciousness of the paradoxic It-reality and Thing-reality. From such symbolizations, I distinguish concepts as definitional formulations referring to objects which have existence in time and space. For instance, you cannot have a concept of history, because history is not really in time and space for it involves the future and we have no knowledge of the future. There is no "thing," history, about which one can talk at all, as we can about this table existing in time and space. The question can then also be raised concerning the existence of finite symbols in mathematical form which perhaps are more than that ... The mathematical form of the universe is a symbol. However, mathematics is a not sufficiently explored problem, and so I cannot give you a definite answer. One simply has to explore the matter historically, mathematically; and I am not going to do this.

So symbol is to be understood in the sense I have mentioned. As far as one can see, a symbol like the beginning of the universe or the universe itself, and so on, is not a concept of anything, but the symbolization of the tension of experience and existence: in time, we exist in relation to the Beyond and so on. As soon as we turn to the Thing-reality, we hit upon the problem that Thing-reality is ultimately not an entity at all, but part of an entity which is a whole, and the whole can only be expressed in symbols. There's no use trying to impose any doctrines or dogmas; we can only work on the basis of what we know at present, making use of the empirical sciences.

On the problem of using symbols to descriminate normatively between true and false, good and bad:

If you ask this question in the face of a given symbolization such as the "big bang," you can say that taking into account the issues connected with symbols and symbolization yields the insight that the complex to be dealt with is superior to any unanalyzed formula such as the "big bang." There is an objective criterion in the question. When you can raise these questions that make sense, then we have improved the problem. When physicists, for example, look for a unified theory, we can raise reasonable doubts whether unified theories in that sense are possible, because the physicist is not dealing with a kind of object from which he is removed. Then we have improved the problem objectively. This is a response in terms of concrete cases; you may have other cases in mind that you may want to bring up.

In response to further questions along the same lines:

You can't get any new facts about the universe as a whole, because the whole is already a symbol, and you can't get a new fact about a symbol.

Take, for instance, the question of the beginning. The issue of the beginning of the beginning exists as far as we have any records. The reason why the records exist is that in time someone can always put the question, What came before this? What came before that? and so on until you run into the problem whether the time-line running indefinitely into the past makes sense: one thing caused by another. Obviously, it is a question about sense or meaning. Where does such a line originate? And the question of origin is independent of the state of knowledge of time-events in the future.

The question concerning the beginning is always the same. Only if we insist on taking a particular state of knowledge—say, a Hebrew state of knowledge, a Greek state, or a modern or early modern state—and extrapolate that as an absolute, you get into a mess. This problem was formulated already by Augustine, who advised his fellow Christians, "Don't talk about physics on the basis of the Old Testament, because there are pagans who are intelligent enough to know more about these things than you do. If you use the Old Testament as a source of knowledge about physics, you make yourselves ridiculous and breed contempt for Christianity." Such tactics are not unknown today. If you go into doctrinization of particular events, then you are wrong; but if you ask the general question about the beginning, you are always right.

The problem as formulated by Augustine is interesting, because if you notice in today's newspapers about the so-called creationist controversy between biologists and Christian fundamentalists, you can see it goes on just as if nothing had happened.

This raises another problem. It is a certain kind of limited intelligence that does such things—a constant in the history of mankind: what Plato and Aristotle called a <u>plethos</u>, the mass civilization problem, no matter what the age. This is just on the empirical side of the issues.

In response to the question about the relation of the prophetic and the philosophical:

There is no such thing as an absolutely prophetic event. The prophetic means a certain insight into reality which is both luminous and intentional, and is given a very compact form by the prophets of Israel. The question whether, say, Hesiod is a prophet or not cannot be decided in the abstract, but only very concretely. Because he deals with the same sorts of problems as the prophets of Israel (ethical, and so on), but only in a more or less compact form. So there is no hard and fast distinction between prophetic and noetic thinking, because we can also say that Plato was a prophet. In the <u>Laws</u> he explains that the divine reality is a matter of vision: <u>opsis</u>.

There is no simple noetic form, because the noetic form is the searching part of a tension in which we search for something to which we are moved to search from the other side—it would be the prophetic or pneumatic part. However, if you distinguish the poles, then you want to talk about the searching and the being moved to search (distinguishing the noetic and the pneumatic) and pretend that you search without being moved to search, or you are receiving information from the movement without searching. Then you get into one-sided prophetism or one-sided noeticism, which in fact does not exist anywhere.

On whether prophets seem not to be so much searching for as in possession of the truth:

One has to determine whether the prophet is more or less educated. We can say that people are prophetically moved but are also limited and restricted in their knowledge or horizon, and then they will talk nonsense, inspired nonsense; you can get that.

On whether common understandings are possible despite historical change:

That they are impossible is simply not true. Because all the categories which I have developed here--for instance, the title of my first chapter, "The Beginning of The Beginning"--have not been invented by me. It is the formula which Aristotle uses for his epistemology in the Analytica Posteriora, second part, last chapter. He was dealing with the continuum problem. If you have a post in a history that is post, then also a beginning of the Beginning. The same is true for the Beyond. There is not just talk about the Beyond. The Beyond was a technical term developed by Plato in the Republic and the Phaedrus as the Beyond of the being-things. Therefore, there is a section in my book about the being beyond being. That is also a problem in the history of mankind that is faced in the compact form of speculation and has been differentiated into different forms up to the present. So there are constants which are historical constants and which involve no relativism or anything like that.

Since every story starts in the middle, you must have a plurality of middles. If you have a plurality of myths, there are also the constants which arise out of the structure of consciousness, so that there is no relativism in talking about the beginning of the beginning.

Every analysis of this form (or every analysis simply!) can lead to misunderstanding if it falls into hands of people who aren't very bright. Absolutely, the non-brightness of the people who might read you is a fact you have to face.

We just have to put up with the fact that there are people who are not sufficiently literate to handle the problems with which we have to deal. I have always had to explain to the students at the beginning of my seminars all my life: there is no such thing as a right to be stupid; there is no such thing as as a right to be illiterate; there is no such thing as a right to be incompetent. It is usually taken for granted you have a right to be all these things, and will still be regarded as a wonderful person.

We always have to recognize this structure, as occurs in Plato's and Aristotle's construct of the plethos, besides the spoudaioi. There are different terms in existence for this structure, which have been supressed again in an incompetent environment of political scientists who don't read Aristotle, outside of the Politics.

On the relationship between philosophy and theology:

There is no simple breach. You might say that philosophy is a term that has been developed by Greek thinkers as a name for their activity of dialectical and analytical exploration of reality. In that connection it became clear that among the realities to be explained was the experience of the gods. The result of this exploration was called theology. You could get into discussions about whether one should reserve the term, theology, for more compact forms of philosophizing like the myths of Hesiod. That is the meaning Aristotle tries to propagate. On this occasion, then, the problem of the myth arises. There is no such thing as myth in the abstract. Myth has become a problem because a compact form of thinking was distinguished technically as "myth" from a more differentiated form of thinking called "philosophy" by Aristotle. That's why we talk about the myths at all; otherwise, there is no talk about myths. The terminology develops as degrees of differentiation develop.

The divorce between philosophy and theology is an historical arrangement. You see, this arrangement was party to deformation. Take, for instance, the problem of religion. For Cicero, for example, religion meant philosophy; and the opposite of religion was superstition in the sense of a primitive fundamentalist mythology. Superstition is compact mythology and religion is the differentiated philosophy: Cicero's definitions in De Natura Deorum. And I cannot improve on that by going into the great question whether religion is derived from the word religare or the word religio—which doesn't mean anything one way or the other. Religio meant what Cicero meant in the context of his sentences. And he meant it to mean: identical with philosophy, in the context of his sentences. More than that we will not say.

If you were to speak of theology in the Christian sense, we would get into problems, because there is no theology in the Christian sense which is not at the same time philosophy, also. And then you might go on to speak concretely, taking as an example the definition of Chalcedon. You can say, "Yes, I believe it because I know the truth intention in it." Or you can say, "My God! You have a dogma of that importance formulated with that second-rate type of philosophy that was in use in the fifth century, as compared to what we know about the matters." It is deplorable, but there is nothing we can do about it, since the dogma was formulated in the fifth century. They use such terms as the nature of man and the nature of God, which I wouldn't use today. Thus, they solve a problem which is an entirely ridiculous problem in theology on the basis of the depositum fidei.

On the truth of the beginning in relation to doctrinal truth:

You cannot simply say "experiences of the beginning." There is one experience of the Beyond which led to the term, Beyond, because and when the Beyond of the being-things is differentiated. Then you can consider, for instance, the Amon Hymns of the twelfth century B.C. (at the same time as Moses), which try to confer on the god, Amon, the qualities of the God beyond the gods--to do so on a less differentiated form of the Beyond. But before you can speak intelligibly about these things, you must have the Platonic concept of Beyond. Otherwise you simply have recourse to the oddity that in the mythology of Egypt you suddenly have Amon becoming superior to all others, the beginning of all the others, and so on.

A similar problem comes up in the <u>Timaeus</u> of Plato, where the Demiurge produces the other gods: a reconstruction which perhaps runs parallel and would be taught by Plato. He insists that the Demiurge produces the other gods and that the other gods are therefore legitimate. But he always distinguishes between the star gods and the gods of tradition, who are the Olympian gods—second rate gods as compared to the star gods.

Plotinus several centuries later has the same problem: that the traditional gods are still preserved, though one really doesn't want them. But for historical reasons, they are still there, and one has to accept them. The gods die, but there is no reason why they first came alive.

On whether the gods serve a useful function:

The gods have no uses. The gods aren't prophets.
There you get into the very profound problem of why God created the world in the first place instead of keeping quiet. This was also a problem known by Catholic philosophy since Empedocles, who was therefore of the opinion that creation was a disturbance of a quiet state in which one is happy; and when the final conflagration at the end of things comes, then at last there is the perfectly ordered hierarchy. Then we are happy.

The problem recurs in the Gnostics of the second century in dealing with the question of the different solutions for the different types of people. The pneumatics, spiritually inspired, will go to the real beyond of the God of the Beyond. Psychics go into paradise; and the somatics will live as they do now, only without the tensions which cause their anxieties. With tensions you cannot be happy.

On whether propositional truth necessarily kills the tension:

It's one way of killing the tension, but it's also one way—since language is still language in all Thing-language—of preserving things. Only we should understand that there are no things; otherwise you get into difficulties. If you construe the beginning of the world and the beginning of time by saying the world began in 4004 B.C., and such nonsense, then you get into difficulties. But that doesn't mean the problem of the beginning of the world is nonsense.

On 'phronesis' in Gadamer:

I'm not sure to what point in Gadamer you are referring. I myself have written on phronesis in Anamnesis. What I understood—here I am not too sure what Gadamer has to say about it—is that Aristotle is clear about the fact that you arrive at concrete decisions on the basis of insights which are not concrete. The result of insight cannot be deduced. It is an analytical account of the ability to arrive at practical solutions in the concrete case. I don't know whether this is the same way Gadamer handles it.

On whether this 'phronesis' tradition may have been lost or deformed:

Perhaps it is not differentiated enough to be generally understood. It would be an everyday problem, the question of having to make a decision on something that is unanalyzed into something that becomes an analyzed decision with an end mediated by explanations or perhaps I should say opinions. It is not always a masterpiece of analysis. One tries to explain how one gets from the nondoctrinal law to the concrete decision.

On Voegelin's technical term, reflective distance:

Let's start from a concrete situation: the Platonic tension of existence between God and man, between perfection and imperfection, between action and insight, and so on—it is metaxy. Now we are living in the tension, just as we were saying about the situation of phronesis. After you have analyzed the situation of phronesis, you know just as much about it as you did before. You have to come from beyond into the concrete situation which is the exact way that we exist. But the difference is, you know that this is the problem and you have a language for it. Now when you find a language for it and you analyze it in a chapter called "Phronesis," then you are speaking about it in a reflective distance from the actual act of phronetic decision which you have to make on your own. And arrival at a dialectical analysis can prevent you from making mistakes about the process in understanding the process, but it doesn't solve the problem. You still have to make the judgment.

On whether Hegel makes the distinction between truth and ideology impossible:

It is worse than that. It is the desire to pretend that Hegel's analysis is a final decision, to come back to phronesis; that when he has analyzed consciousness, then the conflicts of consciousness are resolved. Hence, the works of Hegel, especially the Logik, will replace, for instance, all the Old and New Testaments as a sacred scripture. So there is a libidinous background in which one tries to become a second Christ, which was common at the time. There is Fourier, Saint-Simon, and Comte—everyone wants to be the new Christ; and Hegel was one of them.

On whether what is ultimately wrong with Hegel is his scientizing reductionism of what he presumed to be mythological material:

Yes, you can say that. But then you get into difficulty with mythology, because a myth is not necessarily a misconstruction. What I have tried to bring out is that all the fundamental symbolisms of Plato appear in Hegel, but transformed in such a manner that what comes out is no longer a revelation of a search, but a manipulative finding of the truth; what we would call today, informational communication, which in its easiness and clearness distracts from the understanding of reality—the reduction of reality to informative material.

On the attributes Romantic and Enlightenment as they come up in an analysis of Hegel:

This distinction between Enlightenment and Romanticism is probably invalid. You might call Enlightenment a period of Romanticism; and you might as well call Romanticism a period of enlightened knowledge. The Enzyklopedie of Hegel is an encyclopedia because there is already an Encyclopedie francaise as what gives it legitimacy.

On whether Hegel's or all subsequent German thought—Heideger's as trying to get behind the Enlightenment, for instance—can be placed in the same stream of thought:

Any attempt to get behind something is an attempt to falsify facts. We cannot overlook that certain facts are always real. That was a general problem which also came up in the Enlightenment of the eighteenth century.

We might also include the conception that there are secondary realities and primary realities; or the Lockean conception—all are enlightened attempts to destroy reality. This does not mean that if you try to resist them you are always right. In Goethe, for instance, you have the Farbenlehre in opposition to the Lockean and Newtonian doctrines. It is perfectly correct in seeing the problem, but the assumption that the Newtonian theory of optics is wrong is of course untenable; Goethe's right-minded resistance does not make the positive teaching of his Farbenlehre right. But he did resist the destruction of reality.

On whether, within the mythopoiesis of the 'It' with its formative parousia and pneumatic response in which people respond in part by expressing, any historical and social explication can avoid being magical:

It is spelled out, for instance, in the conceptions of history. You frequently find it said today that our conception of history is Europo-centric. Of course it isn't. But there is something to that accusation. Any interpretation of history which includes the various civilizations and takes account of them was achieved in Europe, beginning with the Greeks—not by the Chinese or the Indians, but in Europe, by the Greeks and nobody else.

One can make guesses that the Greek achievement was due to the fact that there you have intelligent people who live in a moderate and climatologically bearable situation without an empire. Where you do get an empire, in China, it was an independent accomplishment. You can say the non-imperial character of the Greek polis was the reason why the priests were confined to the local cults, and there was no priestly group which could develop a dogma with which one could get into conflict, when as an independent person one spoke about the republic. I don't know what more you can say about it.

On what is to be done where so much deformation in the academy and elsewhere abounds:

You have concrete cases, say in the sixteenth century's great so-called wars of religion. What does an intelligent person like Bodin say? He says that the king in such situations of grave civil war would have to be a mystic who doesn't believe doctrinally in the left or right, or Catholic or Protestant dogmas, or at least have an adviser who is a mystic. You have the same problem today. You have all sorts of wild men like Khomeini and so forth who take their dogma to be the absolute; but what they suppress socially through this doctrinal development is the function of the mystic to tell the doctrinal fanatics that there is a religious fanaticism which really amounts to murder. And that is not sufficiently present in the various civilizations affected by dogmatism today.

In brief, understanding the problem of mysticism as the simple doctrinal understanding of <u>phronesis</u> would be desirable as a task for educators today: reading Bodin's <u>Lettre a Jean Bautru</u> (of 1563) as a fundamental text in every university of the future, which every student must learn.

On the problem of recovering the experiences of mysticism:

We recover them through education. There is a readiness even in such very questionable movements as the Hippie movement in the sixties and seventies. When I first went through the Stanford bookstore, I saw that the two sections which were enormous in comparison to all the others were the section on Religion and Mysticism (<u>The Book of Changes</u>—<u>I Ching</u>—and such stuff) and the section on Pornography. These were the two most voluminous sections in the Stanford bookstore. This has changed: the Pornography section has receded and the section on Mysticism has increased.

Now why do so many want to read that <u>Book of Changes</u>, which is technically an extremely difficult, compact form (I couldn't tell you what the worth of it is)? Because these students, poor devils, are looking for something which they don't get in Sunday School, or the universities. Nobody tells them that it would be a good idea to read, for instance, Meister Eckhart or the <u>Cloud of Unknowing</u>. That is the practical situation: what can we do to tell the college personnel to tell the students not to read <u>The Book of Changes</u>, but the <u>Cloud of Unknowing</u> or Meister Eckhart? It's as simple as that.

I got into these problems of mysticism as a teenager, not because of religious education in school (I went to a Protestant Sunday School), but because Hindus came to give lectures. But one must get it from somewhere. And if you are systematically prevented from getting information about these things, then you are stuck.

On whether the act of remembering as described in the original Foreword to 'Anamnesis' is what Voegelin means by knowing:

I would go even farther than that and claim that this symbolism of remembrance—and again, it was developed in a differentiated way in the <u>memnosyne</u> of Hesiod—doesn't mean only recollecting something that has happened, but, in a sense that has become archaic, to remind somebody of who he is or what he is. Then you get the problem in Hesiod, for instance, that the gods have to be reminded by the Muses that they are gods in spite of all the problems they get into in governing the creation. The gods are in doubt about their nature....

On presence in relation to remembrance and forgetting:

Parousia means presence and you remember this presence by speaking it out: where the name of Christ is pronounced, there he is present. But you have to be reminded you are in Christ, and pronounce it right. It is quite possible that the formulation of the Eucharist as 'in my remembrance' (which is anamnesis) of which Paul speaks always evokes the double-meaning of the remembering of recollection and of remembering in the sense of establishing what the reality is to be.

On whether anything new is constituted by such remembrance:

It depends whether you want to call God new, or whether you want to call his presence new.

On whether the self or the community is newly constituted:

Well, in the new community you have the expressions, sometimes the doctrinal formulae, of the presence of the divine reality in specific ways.

On whether expression is necessary for presence or whether presence of the divine is otherwise operative:

It isn't except through presences: there would be no Christ without somebody who pronounces the Christ and recognizes the Christ in Jesus. You need an objectification in language. Reality is the tensional presence, and language is the way it is the reality; language is a part, a component of the reality.

On whether it is at all proper to speak of language (as either remembered or forgotten) as referring to anything outside itself:

If you introduce that question, you hypostatize the tension. You can't get beyond the fact that you don't see God as an object. God isn't a table.

On whether the It-reality and that which it creatively shapes, say, in the Genesis story, are really distinct:

No, they are not really distinct. These terms are expressions of experienced polarities within our existence. In that sense only are they real. They comprehend us.

Incidentally, since you bring up the matter, I hit on the expression of the It-reality from the extensive discussion of the Es by Karl Kraus in his philosophy of language; he has a collection of several articles on the problem of the Es.

On the nature of the 'It':

Let me formulate it very simply. We are sitting here talking. What is it that moves us?

On whether the theoretic conception of 'creatio ex nihilo' is a derailment:

You get into the difficulty which Augustine and Plato had with this problem, namely, the problem of the projectum in the sense that the Demiurge is creating by operating on the material, and then the recognition that there is no such material. What Plato calls the material, the chora, is always defined negatively—it is not any form. And then in Augustine's theory of creation, you get God, just like Plato's Demiurge, forming things, but forming out of matter without any form.

On whether the notion of 'creatio ex nihilo' does not represent an advance in the differentiation of divine transcendence:

You have two divine symbolisms coming from the Timaeus on which all rely: the creational (the Demiurge) and the salvational. Here the fundamental problem comes up: why does the Demiurge create the cosmos from which God knows who (the salvational God) will have to save all the people? Then you have the peculiar problem that in Plato there is still the predominance of the cosmos as the monogenes: as the unique one, the son of God. And that term, monogenes, is the term which has been preserved in Christian philosophy in the Gospel of John, where it has been transferred from the cosmos to the Christ, from the creational God to the savior-God. This still does not solve the question, Why does the god who produces the world ex nihilo do so in such a manner that it needs a savior? And that problem is never capable of a solution.

Then, of course, you can ask the question, Why is there a story of reality at all?

On whether Plato and Aristotle might not have an adequate notion of divine transcendence:

You could say that, of course, since obviously the salvational aspects were not sufficiently differentiated by them.

On whether, prescinding from the salvational aspect, one mustn't conceive and affirm creation as a free, contingent event caused by a principle that is utterly transcendent:

Yes, you could say it, but it doesn't mean anything unless you place it in the context of some experience.

On whether the paradox of luminosity and intentionality, on Voegelin's interpretation, means that human beings have something within pushing them beyond, but the limit of their experience is always intrinsically conditioned by space and time:

That problem is formulated very well by Plato in the Timaeus where he says that to be in the state of thingness is to be in a state of disorder—anarche. If you would order reality, you would have to have ordered thingness. But things don't want to be in order, they want to be perfect. And Plato has no solution for getting out of this aporia. One can't get out of it.

There is an order that is an imperfect order. It can be made perfect only by abolishing the disorderly character inherent in thingness; and when we abolish thingness, there is nothing to be ordered.

On Stoicism as a response to the distress of disorder:

Stoicism is one relation to it. If you take a representative Stoic such as Marcus Aurelius, he was always of the opinion that you have to conform to the orders of the cosmos: you cannot achieve superperfect logical arrangement of reality, because there are always too many obstacles on account of the needs, passions, stupidity of man, and so on. By about the age of forty, one has understood that pattern of a desire for conformity as regards the laws and the impossibility of achieving perfection, and the constant need for compromise. By the age of forty you know everything about it. The only solution is, you get disgusted with those who can't do anything with the laws in the face of the obstacles. It's useless.

On whether there might be a more adequate salvational symbolism besides Stoicism:

What other answers can we give? You can figure on suffering injustice to the end—you're not permitted to commit suicide under any circumstances.

On whether a properly human end does not involve passing beyond what's intrinsically conditioned by space and time:

Yes. It is the salvational idea of utopia. Utopia is a thing that can't be realized in space and time. You can bring in the eschatological conception of phronesis, which raises the question of thingness posed by Plato and which has fundamentally two solutions: either you can abolish bodily thingness, and then you have the immortality of the soul; or you don't abolish the bodily thingness, and then you get the doxa problem.

On whether the idea of a Beyond not intrinsically conditioned by space and time is simply an experience:

It can simply be experienced as a tensional pole of your experience. It can never be an experience.

(Together with Paul Caringella, the following formulation was reached in conclusion:) Plato in the Timaeus says you can't talk about the divine things except through the things in space and time in which the divine reality is manifest.

AUTOBIOGRAPHICAL STATEMENT
AT AGE EIGHTY-TWO

Eric Voegelin
Stanford University

Ladies and gentlemen: I am under orders today. I have been told to talk about the motivations for my analysis of consciousness. What were the problems that inspired it? Well, that could fill a volume. I will be selective.

I was educated in Vienna, at the University of Vienna, during the situation of the breakdown of the Austro-Hungarian Empire. Let me explain what that means. Until the breakdown in 1918 the Austro-Hungarian Empire was a country equal in population to the United States. It was really an empire, embracing all sorts of nationalities--Czechs, Poles, Serbians, Hungarians, Croatians, Lithuanians, Germans, and so on. The whole personnel of the empire was a mixture of these various cultures. For instance, at the break-up in 1918, older colleagues of mine who had been in the Chancellery told me that on the morning after the resignation of the emperor the Chancellery was empty, because all the personnel who were Slovaks had gone to Prague, the Poles had gone to Warsaw, the Yugoslavs had gone to Belgrade, the Italians had gone home to Italy, and so on. That is also why, after the First World War, these new seccession states, like Czechoslovakia, Poland, or Hungary, functioned fairly well--the personnel operating the bureaucracies were the bureaucrats of the old Austro-Hungarian Empire. This imperial tradition is still effective today, in the sense that upper Italy, above Florence, is as you know the progressive part of Italy, because the Austrian bureaucracy organized it; but the southern part was neither organized by nor part of the Austro-Hungarian Empire, and so was never organized by bureaucrats from Vienna!

In this Vienna, therefore, all the cultural and ethnic problems of imperial size were concentrated after 1918, as well as in the war years. There has been a certain distortion of the picture of Vienna in recent studies of Vienna's intellectual life concentrating on the so-called Vienna Circle--the circle of people, like Rudolf Carnap and Moritz Schlick, with a positivistic orientation--which was no doubt extremely important. But there were half a dozen other such circles, about which nobody talks today. There was a historical society out of which came people like Otto Brunner, the medieval historian in Hamburg later; there was the art history represented by Dvorak, who had just died, and by Strzigowski, who was still alive, and by their pupils (Wilde, a pupil of Dvorak became director of the Cooper Institute in Rome and emigrated) and others like Emanuel Winternitz, who became the organizer of the new music division in the Metropolitan Museum; and there were economists like Fritz Machlup and Gottfried von Haberler and Alfred Schuetz, who became leading personalities in American economic circles. There was the Institute for Byzantine Music, under Egon Wellesz, who went to Oxford after 1937. There was an institute for <u>Urgeschichte</u> (the history of the Stone Age), whose organizer became a Nazi and also left Vienna after the war. He was minister of education at the time when I was fired, in 1938, and I owe him a certain gratitude, because I had to get his permission to leave the country, to accept a job at Harvard, and he permitted it. So there were a number of such circles. They represented considerable influence, not only of German and Austrian but also of Western intellectuals generally.

At the time when I was a student in Vienna, in the 1920s, there were the influences of Marxism through the Social Democratic Party; Freud was leading the psychoanalysts who were there; along with them there were the art historians, the Byzantinists, the medieval historians about whom I have just spoken. That was an environment. In this overall environment the dominant form or special environment in which I grew up was the Law School, with Kelsen and the neo-Kantian movement, first, of the Marburg neo-Kantian persuasion under Cohen, and later that of Husserl, which developed in Freiburg. From that beginning I started.

In the Law School, my job was administrative law. I had to teach courses on the administrative code, which by the way was very good. (A lot of our present American problems in governing the administration of the country and the bureaucracy could be solved very effectively by adopting the Austrian administrative code of procedure!) From this position I had to get my bearings. The Marxist movements were very strong, as well as the psychoanalytic movement and the Fascist movement. None of them seemed quite satisfactory, because at the same time there were intelligent people around who did not belong to any definite school or sect, but from whom you could learn something about reality--spiritual, intellectual, and so on. A strong influence, for instance, was the circle of Stefan George, today almost forgotten, but extremely important at that time. Men like Friedrich Gundolf (who wrote on Goethe), Paul Friedlaender, and Kurt von Hildebrandt promoted the revival of Plato; also my introduction to Plato came from the George circle. Then, too, there was the prevalent critique of the decadent intellectualism, especially of the Viennese daily press, by Karl Kraus. Every month, of course, I had to read <u>Die Fackel</u> of Karl Kraus, and I became aware of problems of the decay of the German language, which are very similar to the problems of the decay we have today in the English language, due to the press and the media and the destruction of rational language. Besides this, there were the great authors, Doderer and Musil, who had considerable philosophical education; they were able to formulate certain problems such as the concept of 'second reality' developed by Doderer, in his Daemonen, which I have adopted. All of these people were always on the verge. You might say Doderer was perhaps, for a while, very strongly inclined towards National Socialism, but he wrote his notes after he saw what it was; his analysis of National Socialism in the post-war novels is extremely acute, and results in the conception of the second realities which replaced the first realities. So that was the general environment.

Now, out of this environment I was led in certain directions in the 1920s because of my period in America as a Rockefeller Fellow. Here I gained experience from Columbia, and at Harvard, and most importantly perhaps at Wisconsin, because John R. Commons, the labor economist, and other people who later played a great part in the labor aspect of the New Deal were there. I was introduced to American problems and had to study an American civilization, the American 'mind,' which differed substantially from anything I had learned in central Europe about problems of the mind or the intellect. And you might say it was a culture shock! Of course we understand that there is a plurality of civilizations and that the verbal and intellectual developments of the type dominant at this time in Vienna were not the last thing in the world; but there were other worlds, with their traditions, which were quite different according to the background—commonsense culture, religion, mysticism, and so on. And that is the reason why, when I came back after a third year as a Rockefeller Fellow in France where I studied (Lalou, Mallarme, Valery, and so on), the German intellectual development afterwards practically ran off like water from a duck's back. I simply had no sensitivity any more for the particular kind of thinking that was specifically German. So I was still strongly influenced in a positive way by Jaspers, but no longer (for instance) by Heidegger. After the American experiences I was impervious to Heidegger. He did not impress me at all with Sein und Zeit, because in the meanwhile, with John Dewey at Columbia and with Whitehead at Harvard, I was acquainted with English and American commonsense philosophy.

I now had to understand what I wanted to do as a political scientist in the law faculty. When I was about thirty I understood that if I wanted to be a political scientist I had to be able to read the classics of political science. That was when I started learning Greek, because I had not had it in high school. A similar development occurred later when I found out that I could not start the history of ideas with Greece, because there were a few things before that—the Hebrews, for instance, and the Babylonian Empire, and so on. Later I learned Hebrew from a rabbi in Alabama. One has to get the instruments for dealing with the sources. I never learned Egyptian sufficiently well, because here the amount of language is very limited, and you cannot really know more about Egyptians than what the Egyptologists know. Here it is legitimate to have recourse to the experts. But usually, in other respects, one has to learn the languages. In the analysis of the Persian documents of the Achaemenian Empire, all the translations by Hieronymus are so different from each other that you would not believe they translate the same original. You really have to learn Old Persian well enough to be sure of what an Achaemenian document really says. So these language problems are a permanent problem: we always have to learn the languages in order to verify what we find in the sources.

Then there came the decisive point when I was kicked out of Austria in 1938—attended by a very funny incident, which I will report because I want to show you the atmosphere. On the one hand, there was in Vienna, of course, a strong center of Jewish intellectual culture, because ten percent of the population were Jews: the intellectual upper class was determinately Jewish; one was expected to grow up in a Jewish intellectual environment. At the same time, on the other hand, because the Jewish environment was dominant, there was strong antisemitism in Vienna. In 1938 a colleague of mine on the law faculty wrote a book on Fascism, in which he quoted my own study of Fascism of 1936, two years earlier. And every time, he put after my name, in parentheses, 'Jew,' exclamation mark—which was very dangerous at the time, because if anybody was treated worse than a Jew it was somebody who was a Jew and pretended not to be a Jew. So I had to go after that matter and find out what had induced him to do such a thing. And at last I got it out of him: one of the professors in the faculty had told him I was a Jew. It was the professor of Germanic law; I asked him how he had thought that. We had a conversation and for a long while he did not want to come out with how he had found out that I was a Jew. At last he said, "Well, our people are not as intelligent as you are." That is the atmosphere in which things happened. They are very funny. But they are not confined in their funniness to these Austrian or Viennese problems. You have the same problem. Later, in my emigration, I had to deal with an American vice-consul by the name of Smith, a very nice fellow and a Harvard boy. I had gotten an appointment from Harvard. It took some time to get the final confirmation of my appointment there; I was waiting to get my visa. The consul was very skeptical about my appointment, because as he explained it, "From the documents I received, you are not a Catholic, you are not a Communist, you are not a Jew. So why should you have to emigrate? And if you emigrate at all, you must have a criminal record!" That was the American vice-consul. Well, in time the letter from Harvard came, with the signature of Arthur Holcombe, the chairman, consenting to my appointment. I was in; I was one of the boys. The criminal record was dropped. I mention these things to show you how funny it is in detail (if one forgets for a moment the horrible consequences that came about), when you deal with these idiots in these various positions in the political situation.

All these various experiences made clear to me that there was a stratum of stupidity as a relevant social factor—ignorance, illiteracy, stupidity; and that the quest for truth, the philosophical investigation, was a very thin upper stratum in any civilization or society, on any occasion always distinct from massive reactions on the part of the mass of stupid people who surround us. It is nothing new of course; it is an insight you find in Plato, in Aristotle. Thus, in the Aristotelian Politics we find the distinction between the plethos, the mass of the people, who are exposed to the special reaction on the stupid level, for one reason or another; and the spoudaioi, the very few mature people who maintain the civilization. If the establishment of the spoudaioi is disrupted by external events, then the civilization breaks down very rapidly within a generation. And that is the problem we have to deal withh in various contexts, now internationally: when certain disruptive events occur, civilization breaks down, and the plethos in the classical sense—the mass of passionately directed people who are more or less illiterate and who do not know what they are doing—come to predominate.

Such phenomena are frequent; you find them frequently; the whole problem of the origin of Greek philosophy and of apocalypticism in Judaism, and so on, is simply motivated by the fact that expansion of empires, such as the Alexandrian Empire or the Roman Empire, destroys the ethnic community in which people live. They are thrown out of their positions of power and are no longer in control of the organization of their own lives; they become alienated from reality, and so engage in all sorts of speculation for saving themselves from their situation, frequently reacting with violence. This problem in the time of Plato can be seen when, in the Laws for instance, he recommends what today would be considered a very liberal policy: that when one Greek polis conquers another, it should not kill on that occasion more than fifty percent of the population. That was a considerable improvement on the actual facts, where one hundred percent of the population were murdered unconscionably. So the legal suggestion is, do not kill more than fifty percent. More—that one should leave perhaps more people alone, and not murder them at all—even a Plato would not dare to suggest.

The same problems occur everywhere. Today we do not have the imperial expansion of Alexander or anything like that, but instead revolution caused by the so-called industrial revolution—large-scale organizations on the level of the division of industrial labor—that exposes the people engaged at the lower level of the process (in manual work, or secretarial work, and so on) to dependence on organizations far beyond their reach; and they can be all of a sudden dismissed because it is no longer possible, for economic reasons, to maintain such an enterprise. Then, when some fellow who has been employed for twenty or thirty-five years is thrown out or becomes unemployed without any fault of his own, he can either resign or be quiet; or he can become violent. Violence is a normal reaction on such occasions. Even if the majority do not become violent, but there are enough people, a few hundred or a few thousand who are of the violent kind, they can organize the rest to support them. Similar problems arose in Germany after the First World War, with the long process of reparations, which exhausted Germany completely and produced enormous unemployment and a decline in the standard of living, with the result that somebody aggressive like Hitler and his friends can instigate a mass agreement to violent reaction. I saw a similar problem growing in 1976 when I was in Teheran. The people I knew belonged to the middle class and were capitalist types: architects of universities and men of this kind. Everybody talked about the corruption at the core and the exploitation of the country through the corrupt members of the royal family and their friends. Now when such talk is general and openly divulged to an outsider, something is very wrong, and you can frequently suppose something is going to happen. And, of course, it did happen, because that sort of corruption was prevalent: for instance, the Iranian automobile company was in the hands of the royal court and its friends, and it made enormous profits because an enormous duty was imposed on imported cars so that everybody simply had to buy a car produced by the Iranian company. Such things were perfectly well known by everybody, and everyone knew who stole what, and so on. At any rate, then, when such disruptions of a traditional form happen—and they happen all the time—then you get the violent reactions.

The question therefore emerges: how far does the function of reason and responsibility go? In this regard, Max Weber distinguished between the ethics of responsibility and the ethics of conviction. He had been faced with the problems of 1918-1919 when he was active in Heidelberg. He had to deal with young men, all of whom had become ideologists of one kind or another, either Fascists or Marxists or Communists or whatever. He tried to influence them and get them away from the ideologies, by explaining to them that they were responsible for the consequences of realizing their ideas. If you have a conviction, for example, that all capitalists must be murdered, you are responsible for the murder of the capitalists, whatever happens afterwards. This appeal, however, was ineffective, because emotions are so strong. We talked last night about the problems of the inspired idiot: when one gets an inspiration that one is on the just side, one feels no concern about consequences of nonsensical, even murderous actions; it is as if one no longer really effects the murders one will be committing.

The point here, then, is that this reality of murdering through inspired idiocy was a fundamental problem that induced me to deal with experiences of the social structures within which human experiences move, and the results of them. We might take as an example of the role of social structure the current Central American problems, which are being managed in various ways, due to the simple fact that Latin American countries are former colonial societies. In the structure of a colonial society, an irresponsible upper class exploits human and material potentialities without taking responsibility for the integration of the society. When, for instance, the lower class increases sufficiently, through demographic development, to the point that the instruments of production, in this case the fertile land on which they subsist, is no longer there, then what should they do? They have no possibility of doing anything, because they have no education; they cannot read and write. One way out is to take arms from whom they can obtain them, and start shooting. But the problem really lies in the structure of the colonial society and its aftereffects, not in communism or capitalism, which are entirely secondary phenomena; and that problem cannot be solved by formal intervention or whatever. The colonial structure is there.

Concrete experiences like this motivated the direction in which my research headed, and I should perhaps say the strongest influence is my perhaps misplaced sensitivity towards murder. I do not like people just shooting each other for nonsensical reasons. That is a motive for finding out what possibly could be the reason someone could persuade somebody else to shoot people for no particular purpose. It is not simply an academic problem, or a problem in the history of opinion and so on, that evokes my interest in this or that issue in the theory of consciousness, but the very practical problem of mass murder which is manifest in the twentieth century. It is a very crucial issue, that if one looks at the history of the twentieth century (say, in the <u>Cambridge History</u>), one finds that this century comes under the era of violence. This is almost the only description that can be given, since here various developments come to a crucial explosion.

Of course, the effectiveness of any analysis is quite limited. Let me give you an example. One of the great problems in the Vienna of the 1920s was of course the race question: antisemitism, antipathy between gentiles and Jews, violence, and the rise of National Socialism. As a political scientist I had to deal with the race question. In my two books on the race problem, I worked and found out and published that the race idea was formulated as such in the eighteenth century. The formulation used in the sources was racial differences. At the same time, the question of evolution was under discussion (the topic of evolution includes the problem of the races, the lesser or lower races, or the better or higher races, and so on). The theory of evolution was analyzed very well in the eighteenth century, especially by Kant. As he explains, you cannot develop a causal theory of evolution, because evolution is evolution of reality as a whole. You cannot proceed by logical analysis from one species to another without knowing where one species develops out of another. You can only say that in fact it does occur. You can go back within the biological sphere to the vegetative level pre-existing animal evolution and state the fact that there is an evolution on the level of the vegetative. And then you can go back to before the vegetative realm, to the material levels which are the basis for the evolution of the vegetative. The vegetative are the basis for the evolution of the animal realm and the animal realm ultimately of the human realm. You can do all that and still not know how all that happens. What is the original force that structures reality and imposes structure on reality? This analysis supplied by the Kritik der Urteilskraft sustains the judgment that a theory of evolution is technically impossible, because evolution implies the mystery of a structuring reality. One should not think, however, that once this analysis is made, it has any influence on anybody. It does not. Neither did Kant have any influence on anybody in this respect, nor did my analysis of this matter of the history of the race idea have any influence on anybody in this respect. If you read through the newspapers today you still find that there are, on the one hand, creationist conceptions of the creation of man, represented by a certain conservative fundamentalist Christianity, and, on the other, the biological conception of evolution in nature. But this is not so, because that the structures appear is just a mystery. We do not know why. In the present discussion of the issue, for instance, as to whether the creationist theory or the evolutionary theory should be put into a high school text, there is still the same level of stupidity as what you find in the 1920s and the same level of stupidity as you find at the time of Kant in the eighteenth century. So nothing happens in practice, even when the problem gets analyzed. One must not expect a rational analysis to make people intelligent all of a sudden. They remain as stupid as they were before.

One may ask what evolution is in the historical sense of the evolution of ideas. When I came to America I was asked by Mr. Morstein-Marx at Harvard to write a brief history of political ideas for McGraw-Hill. I thought it was a good idea. One could do that. There were standard histories of political ideas, which one could imitate to produce a textbook of two hundred and fifty pages without much difficulty. But I was interested in the subject matter; I worked with the sources. It was a mistake. I found out that the standard history of political ideas was George Sabine's, beginning with classical antiquity and working (with a few gaps in the middle ages) up to the modern period. Well, I found out that this procedure would not do, because, besides the predominant classical ideas, there were also a few Christian ideas which did not just fall from heaven, but which were historically connected with the development of Judaism. And Judaism, too, did not just fall from heaven, but was connected with reactions of certain tribal groups to Egyptian surroundings and cosmological-imperial constructions. At that time the Chicago Institute of Oriental Studies and the development of the theory of empires and so on were flourishing, and I included that material. That material increased, and instead of a short history of ideas, all of a sudden there was a manuscript of several volumes. I worked myself all the way from the Chicago Oriental School on the oriental empires up through the nineteenth century. Then I arrived at Schelling and his philosophy of the myth.

That brought the crash. Because Schelling was an intelligent philosopher, and when I studied the philosophy of the myth, I understood that ideas are nonsense: there are no ideas as such and there is no history of ideas; but there is a history of experiences which can express themselves in various forms, as myths of various types, as philosophical development, theological development, and so on. One has got to get back to the analysis of experience. So I cashiered that history of ideas, which was practically finished in four or five volumes, and started reworking it from the standpoint of the problem of the experiences. That is how <u>Order and History</u> started.

From this point on, I had to work until I found that one has to develop these analyses of consciousness, which I am trying to do now in the final volume, in order to bring out the complexities of symbolism. There is no single idea; one cannot write a history of the space idea, a history of the time idea, a history of the soul, a history of matter, a history of this or that, because all these ideas are parts; they are poles in the tension of complexes, and the tensions of complexes are the constants which always recur, from antiquity as far back as written records go and even farther back to the archaeological periods, right up to the twentieth century. I have tried to work out these constants in the last (that is, the fifth) volume of <u>Order and History</u>. From it, I have shared with you the first part of the problem of the Beginning of the story, which introduces the problem of a Beyond of the Beginning of reality, because there is a tension with the It-reality about which the story is to be told; and the story must have an end. The story does not have an end; we are in the middle of an unfinished story. We start in the middle of the story and we stop in the middle of the story where the Beginning of the end is the Beginning. Consequently, the meaning of history--say, the sense of meaning that could be attached to something we call history--does not exist at all. The concept of history of which meaning may become a predicate--the meaning of history--is a concept that arose in the eighteenth century and has been explained in very good recent studies. Until the eighteenth century, history was always the history <u>of</u> something. History which is not the history of something is a new invention; similarly, revolution, which really is only revolution of something, and freedom, which is really only freedom from something, are new ideological <u>topoi</u> of the eighteenth century. They are deformed from analytical concepts, and now are the great topoi about which everybody talks, and which are used without any awareness of the deformation.

So perhaps that is as far as I want to go for the moment in recounting the various steps in my motivation. Now I am quite free to answer questions.

QUESTIONS AND ANSWERS

Question: Professor, did you at one point participate in any economics seminars with von Mises or von Hayek? And what effect did that have?

Voegelin: Sure, I was with von Mises.

Question: And what effect has that had on your work?

Voegelin: Well, the effect, for instance, was that I know that what people usually call inflation isn't inflation, but something else. It is very important to know things like this.

Question: What is inflation then?

Voegelin: Inflation is the increase in monetary means to which no economic productivity-increase corresponds. In this country now we have an entirely different problem. For instance, when prices go up, it is usually called inflation. Actually, though, they don't go up because of an inflation of the monetary means, but because, say, the OPEC cartel raises the prices of oil. If you raise the prices of something, the prices go up, but it is not necessarily inflation. Inflation comes about on account of something different. If, after the prices have gone up for cartel reasons, you go on pretending they haven't gone up for that reason and that you are as rich as you were before; and then continue paying the same salaries and wages as before, then you have inflation. What causes inflation are the high salary levels to which no productivity corresponds because the productivity has actually been reduced on account of the price rise on the part of the cartel. It is also caused by Reagan's economics. This is now gradually being realized by workers who are finding out that they cannot keep on getting the wages they had gotten formerly, because the energy prices are so high--not for inflationary reasons, but because of adaptations needed in relation to the energy prices.

Question: Is this connected with the displacement of traditional societies and cultures by industrial society and culture?

Voegelin: Yes. It is one of the side-effects. Once you have internationalization, you get political influences like the OPEC cartel.

Fred Lawrence: You have suggested that social structures connected with the rise of the division of labor broke down the myths, and community-solidarity and plausibility structures of the prior culture. Now, do you envisage any way forward, by way of replacement, since I know you're not advocating the dismantling of industrial development?

Voegelin: No. There are no solutions to certain problems. For instance, a lot of the problem is that the alienation from processes that are participated in accidentally and merely organizationally (like being a cog in the wheel, and so forth), arouses many different responses. Durkheim, for example, in a quite logical way assumed that the division of labor would offer many opportunities to different abilities, ignoring the problem that different abilities to press a button are not as much of an ability as one might have expected.

When you go to the oil company or a credit union, and see there a board of buttons opposite two chairs in which two gentlemen are seated who look at this board; and every once in a while, one gets up and pushes a button, and sometimes the other one does so--you can imagine the boredom!

This emptiness, however, is not necessarily a disaster, because a lot of people are most happy with that sort of thing. It doesn't disturb them at all. But there are others who are disturbed--the so-called intellectuals--and there are a lot of them. Among the intellectuals there always will be the activists who are not satisfied in a situation in which you can do nothing and want to do something. So then you get the whole development such as the mass development of behaviorism under the aspect of the revolution of society, but with the added fact that no behaviorist has ever been responsible for bringing about a solution. They are only in the universities; but there, too, of course, they are quite unhappy about the situation, because nothing beneficial is ever accomplished within the confines of the university.

Lawrence: How would you distinguish your whole undertaking from that of Jaspers? There are so many similarities in numerous ways: the philosophical faith, the influence of Schelling, the political concerns, and so forth. Would you contrast yourself with him?

Voegelin: Well, I wouldn't necessarily draw too much of a contrast. I frequently attended his lectures in Heidelberg, and my only objection really to Jaspers is that he's so prolix in his writing that it is difficult to find out what he really intends.

James Bernauer: I wonder if you would be willing to compare your project with Hannah Arendt's? I have been struck by the similarity in background you share, and in many ways the similarity of what you identify as significant crises. And yet, I note from one of your pieces in 1953, in which you criticized her interpretation of totalitarianism, that you obviously saw a significant difference in the solution.

Voegelin: Well, I can formulate first the parallel in our upbringings. When I saw her library in New York, she had practically the same books on her shelves as I had on mine. We had read the same things. But there is one great difference: she has an original inclination towards Marx. And my analysis of the philosophy of experience as well as my critique of ideologies, especially of Marxism, simply went against her grain. That Marxism should be nothing but a questionable sectarian movement ... ran counter to her sense of propriety.

Bernauer: If I recall correctly her response to you and your critique of The Origins of Totalitarianism, Arendt felt that your way of approaching the integration of philosophy somehow lost the specificity of the different historic moments. For example, your account of the modern period (in contrast to hers) is not very specifically broken down into the combination of factors—the relatively autonomous realm of the industrial, as well as the breakdown of thought. I always had the sense that you conceived of a certain Weltanschauung movement that she would argue strongly against.

Maybe I can specify this in terms of the problem of race. You devoted two books to it and, of course, in The Origins of Totalitarianism, Arendt took up anti-semitism. She rejected the significance normally placed upon race thinking as opposed to the process of imperialism as an industrial movement. I would be interested if you could address the issue of how race is a factor in the historical development that does culminate for both of you in a murderous situation. How precisely does thought serve? Is it mainly a matter of the articulation of thought? Or is it that thought finds itself in a specific historical dispensation that is involved with the industrial as well as ...

Voegelin: Well, it is a historically complicated affair. We are faced with the fact that civilizations arrive at certain points and not at certain other points. You can take any conception of civilization: oil-based civilization, hydro-based civilization; you can start with the Hebrews, the Indus, in Mesopotamia, on the Yellow River there in China, and so on. And you can then ask why there and why not somewhere else? And you can answer, "Well, because the Chinese, or the Indians at that time, or the Greeks or

Hebrews, or the Mesopotamians are particular, distinct peoples." But what does this mean?

Then the question still arises whether this whole conception of civilization is true. There are always empirical limitations. I found, for instance, when I travelled in Yucatan and Malta for archeological purposes, that such civilizations as that in Yucatan and the Maltan are based on chalk geology. They existed in a geological region where there is not much forest, but just enough of a top soil to maintain their survival. You have a similar situation in Westchester in England--also a chalk-based civilization. They've had to contend with certain consequences, because the rock is of such quality that one could not, for instance, build roads opposite from the soil. In Yucatan, just as in Malta, therefore, the roads are built as sort of levees out of rubble. So these civilizations are older than any of the other civilizations I have mentioned, as may be verified by carbon dating. These neo- or paleolithic civilizations, which are far older than later civilizations, are called the chalk-based civilizations.

One could ask, then, "Is it the rock of the river, or is it the race which was the more crucial for the given civilization?" This was a topic even in Mussolini. Mussolini was always of the opinion that the English are barbarians who were still climbing in the trees when the Romans were a great civilization. That was a racial comment. Are the Romans a superior civilization to the Celts and the Anglo-Saxons?

Bernauer: May I say something specifically about the idea of race in the eighteenth century?

Voegelin: Yes.

Bernauer: In trying to account for the emergence of the idea of race, what would be the line of questioning that you would see as a serious one today? I realize you wrote your book prior to the Second World War.

Voegelin: It came out in 1933. It was immediately suppressed by the Nazis. The next one treating the history of the race idea came out, and about three or four months later, it was destroyed.

Bernauer: Is it a traditional history of ideas trying to account for the emergence of the race idea in the eighteenth century?

Voegelin: No, there are specific reasons: the expansion of science, the history of biology, the observations accumulated from renowned scholars of people's different colors of skin. Buffon's Histoire Naturelle, which gave the first comprehensive classification, made the skin colors the basis of the different races—and of course there are different skin colors. Why there are different skin colors nobody knows. We can do the chemistry, but this still doesn't explain why the different colors.

Of course, there is something to the race problem insofar as biological organization is obviously the basis for intellectual functioning—without brains you cannot work. But how electro-magnetic process in the brain produces thought we do not know. The most you can say for a race theory is that physiological organization co-determines the reactions of people.

Bernauer: Was it a false question? Does the idea of race arise in a specific time and serve a specific political function, a specificity of function, that would perhaps be lost in a panoramic view of history which would see us in a state of derailment? Because of what was a more fundamental experience from the more panoramic perspective, the idea of race would reduce to an example of this more fundamental derailment. But could it be the case that as with Arendt, one could introduce a level of analysis to the idea of race that, in order to do it justice, would have to show its specific function at the time that it appears—in this case, the eighteenth century? I am not sure about the specificity of your reaction to the eighteenth century, since the derailment occurred a lot earlier, it seems.

Voegelin: Oh yes. For every area you can show these deformations of consciousness or of spirit as far back as we have records of history. But at some specific time, problems become acute for one reason or another.

With the development of the natural sciences, the problem of mathematical priority, and so on, became acute. With the developments in the later period, problems of the development of biology and so on. Such problems were complicated by the revolution, with the assumption that the upper class of France—the revolution is chiefly a French idea... The upper class is obsessed by the revolution, which is carried by a lower class of a different race. Empirically, it's partly true.

Bernauer: Thank you.

Voegelin: I'm not sure I understand your problem.

Question: I was reading some Hannah Arendt, and it strikes me that because of your sensitivity to this mystery which reveals itself and constitutes history, you allow yourself a certain flexibility with regard to events of history, whereas someone like Hannah Arendt—I haven't studied her in depth—doesn't permit herself that kind of flexibility and so remains somehow more bound to the event itself; and that to the extent that Marxism plays an orientational role in her thought, she doesn't permit herself very much flexibility towards the events.

Voegelin: On the Totalitarianism I will make one valid criticism: that she overrates the antisemitism problem and she does not pay enough attention to the division of labor in the development of large-scale capitalism. That's what happens, since really these things are interrelated. One source of the German antisemitism at the end of the nineteenth century has to do with the liberation of the serfs. When the serfs were released from serfdom and made independent farmers, they had to start with land, seeds, and tools to get established. Who pays for that establishment? It is paid for by loans. In eastern Prussia, the loans came mostly from Jews. Since the Jews were the creditors for the farmers, and frequently they had to foreclose because the farmers weren't trained sufficiently for enterprise calculations and they lost their money, there was a very strong antisemitism in eastern Prussia. Did it have basically to do with race?

It is the problem of every peasant liberation. They will result in disaster, because you cannot free peasants by telling them, "You are free!" until they are really free. You must also give them capital to start buying machinery; and where does it come from?

I think she's not sensitive enough to the complexity of the issue.

Patrick Byrne: Still within the eighteenth century, but shifting somewhat, last night you mentioned the development of a series of personages who wanted to be the new Christ. You mentioned Fourier as one. Could you talk about that a little?

Voegelin: No, I don't have any passages in detail, but you can find passages cited in my History of Ideas that show that he considered himself a new Christ.

Byrne: Have you written about Fourier at all?

Voegelin: I've mentioned him, I believe, in the context of Comte, in From Enlightenment to Revolution.

Paul Caringella: I'm almost sure there are some quotations from Fourier there ... now in paperback.

Voegelin: The best work on that whole problem is the great three-volume analysis of Comte by Gouhier, a professor at the Sorbonne. In his work on Comte he set forth the periods of his development.

Caringella: Pat, you had an example last night which might fit in—it's a little bit later than the eighteenth century.

Byrne: Laplace.

Caringella: Laplace. People might be interested in hearing about it.

Byrne: In his philosophical essay concerning probabilities—among other things, this is the famous statement of determinism—it's quite clear that Laplace is systematically replacing the Christian theological virtues of faith, hope, and love by moving them into a context of deterministic mathematics. He starts right off by saying, "The reason I'm writing this is that people are believing things that they ought not to believe, and I'm going to give you a calculus that's going to structure your believing." And about three chapters later he has a chapter called, "Concerning Hope," in which he replaces hope. Or, in other words, hope becomes in effect: "What should you bet on? What's a reasonable bet, and what's not?"

Question: I've heard that you've done researches into the cave paintings in France. Was that a fruitful inquiry, and will your results appear in volume 5 of Order and History?

Voegelin: I don't know yet whether I can include them. These are complicated affairs, with pictures and so on. That is work done chiefly by Marie Koenig, the German archeologist. She has analyzed the principle ornaments and paleographs. The cosmos is structured like an axis. A lot is to be done with it. But hers is the most interesting.

[Editorial note: A section of the tape involving chalk-talk from a blackboard by Dr. Voegelin was not sufficiently retrievable to be included here.]

Charlotte Tansey: I don't know if anything like this came up last night, but could you comment on any developments in your notion of intentionality from Anamnesis to the first chapter of your new book?

Voegelin: Well, I don't know if it's a development. It's just a more accurate description of the complexes; of the problem of complex itself; of the concept of tension (it's better developed); of all these tensions and systems of complexes.

Tansey: But you wouldn't deny anything you said in Anamnesis?

Voegelin: No. I rarely have something to deny because I always stick close to the empirical materials and do not generalize beyond them. So when I generalize, I have to generalize because of the materials.

Tansey: But sometimes you change your stresses.

Voegelin: Yes, one has to change the stresses on account of something one notes in the materials.

Tansey: I was wondering which texts Fred was referring to this morning, whether it was to Anamnesis or the current work?

Fred Lawrence: I took them all together.

Voegelin: I am really in agreement, but I would only hesitate to go beyond the formulation of the tensions and the complexes, because I see no real experiences of anything going beyond that formulation.

Lawrence: I think one way of thinking about our differences would be to begin from your analysis last night in answer to the question about the criterion. Your answer that the criterion for the answer resides in the question would be the same as I (or Lonergan, I think) would give. My approach then would be to go beyond speaking about questions and answers in a generic fashion by noticing real differences specifying the questions that are aimed at understanding over against other sorts of questions.

Your emphasis is to say, "I don't want to talk about what I do not have an experience of." I do not want to discourage or deny that; but when we get insights into data, phantasms, or complexes of experience, that insight is starting to get beyond what is intrinsically conditioned by space and time. Insight is an experience we have; and we pivot, on the basis of the insight, to specify what it is in the data that we have grasped by our insight, in formulating and in conceiving. For example, in geometry, we can understand the difference between a dot which we can see or imagine and a point which we can conceive of as an element in the intelligibility of the circle, but we cannot actually see or imagine it--there is an instance of our conscious intentionality's getting beyond what's intrinsically conditioned by space and time. We are conceiving of the intelligibility of the circle; of what can be verified as such; and yet it is not properly imaginable. Here we get an experiential opening for speaking about what is beyond the realm of bodily things we were speaking about last night with regard to the Timaeus.

Voegelin: Well, you see I would qualify that symbol of insight. I'm not quite happy about it. Insight is a result in your language, as far as I understand you. I would say we can have insights which remain inarticulate ...

Lawrence: Oh, sure!

Voegelin: This is the phronesis problem which we have discussed last night.

Lawrence: Oh, yes, I think that too.

Voegelin: And they precede anything else.

Lawrence: Yes.

Voegelin: And then when you get an analysis of the insight, you find that the insight dissolves quickly.

Lawrence: Oh, I see. Well, it seems to me, then, that's really where we differ. Because when you go from not getting the point to getting the point (by insight or an act of understanding), that is an experientially discernible difference. It's something you experience, and it's not reducible to other experiences outside that. It's not just a result, but an event that supervenes on the tension of consciousness in the process of inquiry when we grasp the point, or better, perhaps, have the point stand out for us in a way that it didn't before.

Voegelin: I can only talk about these things concretely. Let's say God is a symbol resulting from some sort of insight. When I analyzed the problem at the beginning of the interpretation of the sources of the ancients, I find that there are two tensions fundamentally: the creational God and the salvational God. This raises the question: is the creational God the same as the salvational God? If they are the same, then we arrive at the mystery of the divinity which creates the world from which it has to save people. Then the question, 'Why?' arises. This question is answered by constructions: the fall of man, or the fall of God, if you happen to be a Gnostic. You cannot get beyond that.

Lawrence: Just as a question for information, have you done work on the Ignatian mysticism?

Voegelin: No.

Lawrence: Ah. When we were reading your essay on the Beyond in my course on God last semester, I tried to suggest to my students what you were talking about in a context that might be familiar to them, so we took the Spiritual Exercises of St. Ignatius: the tension, the experiences of consolation and desolation, and what Ignatius intends by the 'consolation without a cause'—the difference between that and every other imaginable correlation within the feeling of the tension. It seems to me that once again, here we are talking about something that is experiencable and yet it is clearly beyond. And one can speak about it in a non-paradoxical way...

Paul Caringella: Well, no. You just talked paradoxically. I don't want to put words in your mouth ...

Lawrence: Oh, go ahead!

Caringella: (I'm taking the words from the second chapter.) You just said you have an experience of the inexperiencable. I think that's what you just said.

Lawrence: No, I'm saying that experience ... It's opening up the meaning of experience.

Caringella: Yes, that it includes the experience of something ...

Lawrence: Okay. Yes, 'of something'... What?

Caringella: Beyond. You just used the word 'beyond.'

Lawrence: Yes, beyond ...

Caringella: Beyond what?

Lawrence: Beyond what's intrinsically conditioned by space and time.

Charlotte Tansey: But that's where it seems to me the parallel is more with Lonergan's notion of love, and less with his notion of ...

Lawrence: I'd be happy with that, sure. But I think it can also be done with regard to insight. But I'm happy to go that route. That's the one that involves mystagogy as the center of philosophy and theology, the one that such philosophy and theology would go with.

<u>Voegelin</u>: I'm really not familiar with the matter.

<u>Michael O'Callaghan</u>: Is it ever possible to explain to a violent, murderous society that a non-violent attitude is not also stoical? In other words, if I want to give an alternative to violence without becoming a stoic, what do I say to violent people? Or will they even listen?

<u>Voegelin</u>: I'm not sure I understand your question. You cannot abolish violence altogether, because of the mysterious differentiation of human beings into people who have limited intelligence and people who are not so limited. I do not know what you can do with a violent man who disturbs your existence but to kill him. So violence produces violence. There is the historical account in Tacitus. His father-in-law, Agricola, was a Roman general dealing with two Germanic tribes on the border. There he portrays a speech by Agricola explaining to the Germanic tribe the consequences of a battle, and then a counter-speech by a Germanic chieftain explaining: "Well, if we don't have a place to live, we at least have a place to die." Violence is perhaps unavoidable in such a situation.

<u>Question</u>: You see no hope in the efficacy of intelligent people? There is nothing for the intelligent person to hope for in terms of his efforts with the unintelligent?

<u>Voegelin</u>: Usually, results come when murderous excesses have gone far enough to make even an idiot see that he is not getting anywhere. But that can go very far.

<u>Question</u>: At the start of <u>Order and History</u> I, you discuss what you call the quaternarian structure of reality consisting of God, man, world, and society. I am interested in how that structure fits in with the twofold or threefold paradoxical structure of consciousness discussed in the "Beginning of the Beginning." Do each of the four symbols of the quaternarian structure of reality partake of the paradoxicality of the twofold structure of consciousness as luminosity and intentionality, or is there another sort of relation between them? I am a little confused.

<u>Voegelin</u>: I am too. The problem was just raised: what is an insight? You start from symbols ... and these are the symbols which constantly recur in all political and philosophical analysis since there have been historical records. We have to talk about these things because everybody talks about them without first knowing what they are. But we are already <u>in</u> ...; and this being-already-in is a special problem. We do not think from

scratch, we do not start with a tabula rasa, but we think in terms which we grew up with; and these are such fundamental terms in which all practical problems about symbolizing/thinking about reality is done. Actually, we start the analysis with the formula of reality which we have found in Homer and Hesiod and then goes constantly through the history of mankind: "Reality is ..." Now, what is reality? The things that are, the things that happen, the things that perish. This leads to the question, What are things? And, of course, that includes the gods. You start from somewhere, and then you can work your way around in terms of the beginning.